ACCELERATED LEARNING WORKBOOK

to accompany

Reid

The Prentice Hall Guide for College Writers
Tenth Edition

Michelle Zollars
Patrick Henry Community College

Boston   Columbus   Indianapolis   New York   San Francisco   Upper Saddle River

Amsterdam   Cape Town   Dubai   London   Madrid   Milan   Munich   Paris   Montreal   Toronto

Delhi   Mexico City   São Paulo   Sydney   Hong Kong   Seoul   Singapore   Taipei   Tokyo

Accelerated Learning Workbook to accompany Reid, The Prentice Hall Guide for College Writers, Tenth Edition.

Copyright © 2014 Pearson Education Inc.

1 2 3 4 5 6 7 8 9 10— EBM —16 15 14 13

ISBN-10: 0-321-96187-0

ISBN-13: 978-0-321-96187-7

www.pearsonhighered.con

Contents

Worksheets

Appendixes

Preface

Time is a valuable commodity; as a busy college student, no one knows this better than you. Enrolling in an accelerated English course allows you to reach your goal of achieving a college education more quickly than you otherwise might.

In an accelerated English course, you are co-enrolled in both the pre-college and college-level courses at the same time. The information and skills you learn in the developmental course are contextualized and applied in real time in the college-level course. You realize their use and value immediately as you earn college credit.

Your instructor will guide you in strengthening your reading and writing skills, and when you successfully pass both courses, you will be prepared to take on any college writing assignment!

The *Accelerated Learning Solution for The Prentice Hall Guide for College Writers* in Pearson's MyWritingLab supports reading and writing assignments featured in the book. Additional questions will help you interpret and analyze the readings on a deeper level and help you advance your vocabulary knowledge. New activities will also guide you in thinking and working through the writing assignments from the text.

MyWritingLab also helps you strengthen the grammar in your writing: you begin by taking a Path Builder diagnostic test, receive a personalized set of content modules that form your Learning Path, and complete Skills Checks within each module to determine which topics you've mastered and which need more work. Lastly, the *Accelerated Learning Solution for The Prentice Hall Guide for College Writers* offers tips to help you build academic, life, and professional skills.

A significant portion of the content found in MyWritingLab's *Accelerated Learning Solution* is also available in this *Accelerated Learning Workbook,* a convenient and easy-to-use print format.

Michelle Zollars
Patrick Henry Community College

About the Author

Michelle Zollars, Associate Professor and Coordinator of the Accelerated Learning Program at Patrick Henry Community College, authored the reading and writing support for accelerated courses using *Strategies for Successful Writing.* She has been teaching the accelerated composition model for over five years; has presented on acceleration at the National Association for Developmental Education conference, the Council on Basic Writing conference, and the Conference on Acceleration; and has served on the Developmental English Curriculum Team of the Virginia Community College System.

CHAPTER 3   Observing and Remembering

Activities to Support the Writing Assignment

OBJECTIVE 3.3 *Use collecting strategies to develop a personal narrative.*

1. Think of a memorable incident from your past. It could be something exciting, traumatic, embarrassing, funny, or any other emotion that makes it memorable. Brainstorm for five minutes, writing down any words, thoughts, or images that come to your mind.

2. Think of a memorable incident from your past. Interview someone involved who would remember the story well. Focus specifically on details that you may not be able to recall clearly by yourself. Listen carefully for those details, and take notes during the interview. In the space below, summarize important points from the interview, making sure to include the most important details.

3. Using a story map, interview, or other prewriting activity, write an introductory paragraph for your observing and remembering essay. Make sure to establish who, when, and where. Create a thesis statement that reflects the lesson learned from the experience.

4. Using your interview or other prewriting activity, choose a memorable incident from your past about which you could write an observing and remembering essay. Make a list of the following details you want to include in your essay.

   1. main characters

   2. other characters

   3. conflict

   4. setting

   5. rising action:
      event 1

      event 2

      event 3

   6. climax

   7. resolution

5. Write 3 to 5 possible titles for your essay. Remember that your title should get the reader's attention. Titles can simply be an accurate label or something less direct. Take another look at the titles of the sample essays in the chapter.

Additional Questions for Writing and Discussion for Alejandrez, "Cesar Chavez Saved My Life"

> **OBJECTIVE** *Analyze an essay.*

1. What is the turning point in Alejandrez's story?

   a. when he saw his father bowing down to his boss
   b. when he got a raise on his job
   c. when he started visiting prisons
   d. when he first heard the words of Cesar Chavez

2. In paragraph 6, Alejandrez returns to describing an event that happened in a previous time. This technique is called

   a. flashback.
   b. dominant idea.
   c. chronological order.
   d. contrast.

3. Paragraph 18 uses the word "indigenous." Using context clues, determine a synonym for "indigenous."

   a. native
   b. religious
   c. secret
   d. foreign

4. What type of organization is used in paragraphs 1–5?

   a. chronological
   b. spatial
   c. order of importance
   d. cause and effect

5. What is the author's dominant idea in this essay?

   a. how racism affected him as a child and continues to do so today
   b. how being inspired by someone led him to inspire others
   c. how easy it is to let those in authority have control over one's life
   d. how more needs to be done to help nonviolent criminals

Additional Questions for Writing and Discussion for Petry, "The Wind Catcher"

OBJECTIVE *Analyze an essay.*

1. Petry uses several similes in his essay. Which of the following from the revised version does NOT contain a simile?

    a. paragraph 3, sentence 1
    b. paragraph 3, sentence 4
    c. paragraph 4, last sentence
    d. paragraph 4, sentence 2

2. What is the main idea of the essay?

    a. To Petry, his cowboy hat looks even better today than the day he bought it.
    b. Petry regrets not taking better care of his hat.
    c. Petry wishes he had spent the money on something else.
    d. Petry plans to buy another hat just like this one.

3. What type of collecting strategy most closely describes the notes and details that are listed before the first draft?

    a. clustering
    b. brainstorming
    c. looping
    d. freewriting

4. What is the primary type of sensory detail used in this essay?

    a. touch
    b. smell
    c. sight
    d. sound

5. In comparing the revised version of the essay with the first draft, most of the added details consist of

    a. stories related to the hat.
    b. more information about the day the author bought the hat.
    c. more description.
    d. the author's attempt to have the hat cleaned.

Additional Questions for Writing and Discussion for Bovard, "The Red Chevy"

> **OBJECTIVE** *Analyze an essay.*

1. Which of the following is NOT part of the author's description of her rape and the months that followed?

   a. the physical effects that followed the rape
   b. the reasons that men rape
   c. how the author got help
   d. how old she was when the rape occurred

2. "By late October," "By the middle of November," and "In the end," are all examples of

   a. similes.
   b. metaphors.
   c. sensory details.
   d. transitions.

3. What type of order is used throughout most of the essay?

   a. spatial
   b. order of importance
   c. general to specific
   d. chronological

4. Paragraph 7 uses the term "impervious." Using context clues, which of the following is an antonym (opposite word) for "impervious"?

   a. vulnerable
   b. victim
   c. immune
   d. resistant

5. What is Bovard's main purpose in remembering this event and then telling her readers about it?

   a. to lobby for tougher sentences for sex offenders
   b. to dispel the myths often associated with rape victims
   c. to encourage others who have been through a traumatic experience
   d. to describe the legal process rape victims go through

CHAPTER 4   Reading Critically, Analyzing Rhetorically

Activities to Support the Writing Assignment

OBJECTIVE 4.1 *Use techniques for critical reading.*

1. Find the essay "Cyberbullying" by Jennifer Holladay in Chapter 10. Read the essay and make double-entry notes:

Notes regarding the main ideas and key features of the text	Your questions and reactions

2. Find the essay "Cyberbullying" by Jennifer Holladay in Chapter 10. After reading it, answer the following questions:

    1. What is the rhetorical occasion for this essay?

    2. Who is the intended audience?

    3. How effective is the title?

    4. What is the thesis of the essay?

3. Read the essay "Bullying as True Drama" by Danah Boyd and Alice Marwick in Chapter 10. After reading it, write a one-paragraph summary of the essay.

4. Read "Facebook Wrestles with Free Speech and Civility" by Miguel Helft in Chapter 10. Write a one-paragraph response that interprets and reflects on the text. Explain key passages and how your own experiences, attitudes, and observations relate to the essay.

5. Using an essay, article, or advertisement approved by your instructor, begin prewriting for your summary/analysis/response essay by answering the following questions:

1. Who is your audience?

2. What is your genre?

3. Are you writing a critical summary and response or a rhetorical summary and analysis?

After answering these questions, draft a thesis statement that reflects a clear, overall main idea.

Additional Questions for Writing and Discussion for McGrath, "Rhetorical Analysis of Gregory Petsko's Open Letter to George M. Philip"

OBJECTIVE *Analyze an essay.*

1. What is McGrath's main criticism regarding Petsko's use of pathos?

   a. It has the opposite effect on Philip than what Petsko intended.
   b. The use of fictional characters is childish.
   c. It insults students who might read the letter.
   d. The insulting language is not professional.

2. In paragraph 2, McGrath uses the word "derisive." Using context clues, determine the meaning of "derisive."

   a. academic
   b. complimentary
   c. confusing
   d. mocking

3. According to McGrath, Petsko's appeal to logos is effective in his use of

   a. specific examples for handling financial problems.
   b. real-life application of knowledge.
   c. persuading the public audience.
   d. experience as a classics major.

4. The essay map used by McGrath in this selection is

   a. found in the first paragraph.
   b. revealed at the end of the essay.
   c. found in the second paragraph.
   d. implied, not stated directly.

5. The introductory paragraph summarizes the piece to which McGrath is responding. Using the first paragraph for this

   a. is ineffective because it isn't detailed enough.
   b. would be more effective in the conclusion.
   c. is effective because it incorporates the writer's thesis statement.
   d. is effective because the reader of this essay may not be familiar with the letter.

Additional Questions for Writing and Discussion for Koester and Browe, "Two Responses to Deborah Tannen"

OBJECTIVE *Analyze an essay.*

1. In Koester's essay, she makes the point that the evidence used is one of the strengths of Deborah Tannen's article. What is Browe's opinion of Tannen's use of evidence?

   a. Browe has the same opinion as Koester.
   b. Browe asserts that Tannen's evidence is not convincing.
   c. Browe makes the claim that Tanner does not provide enough evidence.
   d. Browe does not discuss Tannen's use of evidence.

2. Which of the following is NOT one of Tannen's writing strategies that Koester cites in her essay?

   a. evidence
   b. argument qualifications
   c. parallel format
   d. extensive research

3. One of Browe's primary criticisms of Tannen's article is that it

   a. does not discuss a worthwhile topic.
   b. does not have a clear audience.
   c. is not organized well.
   d. lacks focus.

4. What is the purpose of paragraph 6 in Koester's essay?

   a. It states Koester's thesis.
   b. It summarizes the previous paragraphs.
   c. It provides a conclusion for the previous five paragraphs.
   d. It paraphrases Tannen's essay.

5. The thesis of Browe's essay is

   a. stated in paragraph 4.
   b. stated in the introductory paragraph.
   c. the same as Koester's.
   d. not stated directly in the essay.

CHAPTER 5   Analyzing and Designing Visuals

Activities to Support the Writing Assignment

OBJECTIVE 5.1 *Use techniques for analyzing visuals.*

1. On the Internet, view the painting *American Gothic* by Grant Wood. Then, look at the *American Gothic* photograph by Gordon Parks in Chapter 5 of your textbook. Answer the following questions:

   1. What story does Parks' photograph suggest?

   2. Who has the power in Wood's painting? How do you know?

   3. Why do you think Parks chose to give his photograph the same title as the painting, which was painted 12 years before Parks took his photograph?

2. View the drawing *Day and Night* by M. C. Escher in Chapter 4 of your textbook. Analyze the repetitions of shape, and the contrasts of light and dark in the picture.

3. Using magazines or online resources, find an advertisement for a brand of men's or women's cologne. Answer the following questions:

1. Does any text accompany the ad? If so, what is its purpose? If not, is the ad powerful enough without words?

2. What is the focal point of the ad?

3. What claim can you make about the ad's overall effectiveness?

OBJECTIVE 5.2 *Use techniques for designing visuals.*

---

4. Suppose you had to design a poster that shows today's woman and her war-related tasks. Write any necessary text below, and describe any images you would use.

5. Choose a piece of writing you have done either for this class or for another class. What visual(s) could you add to support your thesis? For example, if you have written an observing and remembering essay, you could create a timeline of the entire event or include a photo of the event. Describe your essay and your visual(s) below.

Additional Questions for Writing and Discussion for Lewis, "Some Don't Like Their Blues At All"

> **OBJECTIVE** *Analyze an essay.*

1. The purpose of paragraphs 1 through 10 is to

   a. criticize the advertisements.
   b. discuss how successful the advertisements have been.
   c. describe the stereotypical attitudes society has toward men and women.
   d. give a visual description of the advertisement.

2. The word "BLUES" in the text that accompanies the advertisements refers to

   a. a musical style.
   b. an emotion.
   c. the background color of the ads.
   d. the color of clothing the models are wearing.

3. The part of the essay that describes the advertisements combines comparison with

   a. chronological order.
   b. order of importance.
   c. spatial organization.
   d. cause and effect.

4. The thesis of this essay

   a. is established at the beginning of the essay.
   b. is implied.
   c. is part of the conclusion.
   d. comes after the visual description that ends with paragraph 10.

5. Lewis uses ethos, pathos, and logos throughout her essay. By using ethos, she is trying to

   a. point out the negative stereotypes used in the advertisements.
   b. persuade her readers not to buy FILA clothing.
   c. explain how clothing companies design advertisements.
   d. inform readers regarding how magazines choose layout styles.

CHAPTER 6   Investigating

Activities to Support the Writing Assignment

OBJECTIVE 6.2 *Use techniques for investigative writing.*

1. Using a search engine like Google, investigate this question: How does aspirin prevent heart attacks?

    Write your answer in a way it could be understood by your classmates.

2. Do a little online research on either the major you have chosen or a career field in which you are interested. Write one question for each of the five Ws (who, what, when, where, why) and answer the questions.

3. Using your college library database, find an article about the profession you plan on pursuing. Note the author, title, publication, page numbers, date, and other source information that you would need to create a citation of the source.

4. Create five survey questions that could be used to investigate student use of a dining hall at your school. Review Chapter 6 if necessary before creating your questions.

5. Create a list of eight to ten interview questions you could ask of someone who works in the same profession that you plan to work in.

Additional Questions for Writing and Discussion for Macke, "Permanent Tracings"

> **OBJECTIVE** *Analyze an essay.*

1. What organizational pattern does Macke use in paragraph 1?

    a. chronological
    b. order of importance
    c. general to specific
    d. spatial

2. In paragraph 2, what is the meaning of the metaphor, "I was a suit..."?

    a. Gasket was in jail.
    b. Gasket was a tailor.
    c. Gasket was a professional businessman.
    d. Gasket worked at a job he didn't like.

3. The information in paragraphs 4 and 5 are not in Macke's notes that are found at the beginning of this selection. What investigative technique would she have used to gather this information?

    a. observing
    b. interviewing
    c. researching
    d. questionnaires

4. During the course of Macke's research, she

    a. decided to get a tattoo.
    b. learned about the history of tattoos.
    c. gave questionnaires to Gasket's customers.
    d. changed her opinion of the tattoo parlor.

5. In paragraph 3, Macke refers to Gasket's "code of steel." This is an example of

    a. a metaphor.
    b. a simile.
    c. irony.
    d. an analogy.

CHAPTER 7 Explaining

Activities to Support the Writing Assignment

OBJECTIVE 7.2 *Use techniques for explaining how (process analysis).*

1. Using the topic of how to find a book in your college library, list in order the required steps of the process. Your audience would be a new student who is using the library for the first time.

2. Using the topic of how to find a book in the college library, list one or two statements that provide warnings or ways to avoid problems.

OBJECTIVE 7.3 *Use techniques for explaining why (causal analysis).*

3. Using the topic of college students and drinking, list three reasons why many college students drink and three effects of this drinking.

4. An effective thesis statement for a causal analysis identifies the topic, explains its importance, and often gives a summary. Here is an example:

   "Excessive exposure to the sun causes many health problems; the effects of too much sun are skin cancer, second-degree burns, and heat stroke."

   Write an effective thesis statement for a causal analysis on college students and drinking.

5. Examples are often used in essays that explain what something is or means. Using the topic of stress, brainstorm a list of examples of stressful situations that could be used in a definition essay.

Additional Questions for Writing and Discussion for Orman, "How To Take Control of Your Credit Cards"

OBJECTIVE *Analyze an essay.*

1. Who is Orman's audience for this essay?

   a. people with credit card balances
   b. people with high credit scores
   c. people making over $75,000 a year
   d. people applying for their first credit card

2. Which of the following paragraphs contains a causal analysis?

   a. paragraph 9
   b. paragraph 20
   c. paragraph 14
   d. paragraph 17

3. Which of the following paragraphs explains a process?

   a. paragraph 5
   b. paragraph 12
   c. paragraph 21
   d. paragraph 1

4. Which of the following statements is true regarding Orman's use of informal language?

   a. Informal language is appropriate, given that the article is specifically for a younger audience.
   b. Informal language is appropriate, given that the article was originally written for a popular website.
   c. Informal language is inappropriate, given that finances are a very serious matter.
   d. Informal language is inappropriate, given that the essay is published in a textbook.

5. This explaining essay is primarily a

   a. descriptive process analysis.
   b. prescriptive process analysis.
   c. extended definition.
   d. causal analysis.

Additional Questions for Writing and Discussion for Tannen, "How Male and Female Students Use Language Differently"

> **OBJECTIVE** *Analyze an essay.*

1. Paragraph 12 uses an example of a student who was disappointed in a presentation he did. What type of shaping strategy is used in this example?

   a. process
   b. causal analysis
   c. extended definition
   d. comparison

2. Paragraph 7 uses what shaping strategy in explaining conversational style?

   a. comparison
   b. causal analysis
   c. process
   d. extended definition

3. Considering the subject and the original place of publication *(The Chronicle of Higher Education)*, who is Tannen's intended audience?

   a. college professors
   b. psychologists
   c. college students
   d. foreign students

4. Which of the following is Tannen's primary supporting evidence?

   a. statistics
   b. research
   c. interviews
   d. anecdotes

5. Paragraph 6 uses the word "disparate." Using context clues, what is the meaning of "disparate"?

   a. desperate
   b. impoverished
   c. remote
   d. different

Additional Questions for Writing and Discussion for Blakely, "White Lies: White-Collar Crime in America"

OBJECTIVE *Analyze an essay.*

1. Paragraph 5, sentence 1 reads, "By explaining the human costs behind these white-collar crimes, I hope to show why the public must pay attention to this public scourge." What is the function of this sentence?

   a. It gives an effect of the cause listed in the previous paragraph.
   b. It gives an opposing viewpoint from the main idea of the paper.
   c. It states the purpose of the paper.
   d. It is the first of three parts of the essay map.

2. Refer to paragraph 9 of the essay. What is the primary writing strategy used in this paragraph?

   a. definition
   b. comparison
   c. process
   d. cause and effect

3. Refer to paragraph 6 of the essay. What is the primary writing strategy used in this paragraph?

   a. comparison
   b. cause and effect
   c. definition
   d. process

4. Review paragraphs 6 through 9. Which of the following does Blakely use as a paragraph hook?

   a. "Edward Southerland"
   b. "white-collar crime"
   c. "occupation"
   d. "American"

5. In the essay overview, Blakely comments that his paper is "exigent." After reading the overview and the essay, and considering Blakely's tone in the essay, which of the following would be the correct definition of "exigent"?

   a. is well written
   b. is his best work
   c. requires immediate action
   d. is intended for a specific audience

Additional Questions for Writing and Discussion for Brosseau, "Anorexia Nervosa"

> **OBJECTIVE** *Analyze an essay.*

1. Brosseau's thesis statement in this essay includes her essay map. The two subtopics of the essay map are

    a. lying and depression.
    b. physical and emotional effects of anorexia nervosa.
    c. gymnast and dancer.
    d. weakness and organ damage.

2. What is the primary writing strategy of this essay?

    a. process
    b. cause and effect
    c. definition
    d. comparison

3. Which of the following would be the primary audience for this essay?

    a. teenage girls
    b. parents
    c. psychologists
    d. medical doctors

4. Brosseau uses definition as a writing strategy when she

    a. gives examples of the lies she told.
    b. tells the story of breaking her fingers at gymnastics.
    c. explains what dysmenorrhea is.
    d. lists the various health problems she had.

5. In paragraph 2, Brosseau writes, "By doing this, I lost ten pounds in one week and gained the approval of my peers." This sentence uses the strategy of

    a. cause and effect.
    b. definition.
    c. comparison.
    d. process.

CHAPTER 8   Evaluating

Activities to Support the Writing Assignment

OBJECTIVE 8.1 *Use techniques for evaluating.*

1. Select a restaurant you visit frequently. Write a paragraph in which you evaluate the restaurant on ONE of these criteria: setting, service, or food. If you choose food, write about one particular meal or item, not all the food you have eaten there.

2. Brainstorm a list of the major differences between owning a home and renting an apartment. Then, make a recommendation for which is better for a recent college graduate who has just gotten his or her first job.

3. Visit your college's website. Evaluate its organization and provide support for your evaluation.

OBJECTIVE 8.2 *Use collecting strategies to develop your evaluation.*

---

4. Think of a movie for which you have read the book upon which it is based. Evaluate the movie by comparing it to the book. Make a list of the major differences and similarities between the two, and then write a sentence explaining which was better.

5. Interview someone who has a job in your prospective career field. Focus your questions on the person's opinions and judgments about this career. Write the main points of the interview here.

Additional Questions for Writing and Discussion for Sedaris, "Today's Special"

OBJECTIVE *Analyze an essay.*

1. Sedaris uses sophisticated words when describing the food at the restaurant. What is his purpose in using this type of vocabulary?

   a. to praise the food
   b. to make fun of the food
   c. to educate the reader
   d. to appeal to a particular audience

2. Sedaris uses dialogue throughout the essay. Re-read the sections in which the author is speaking. What is the main purpose of the dialogue?

   a. to help the story move along
   b. to contrast himself with his dinner partner
   c. to express his opinion indirectly
   d. to highlight his knowledge as a food critic

3. Sedaris expresses his opinion throughout the essay in an indirect way. Which of following most accurately gives his overall judgment or claim?

   a. People should try different restaurants in order to expand their dining experiences.
   b. Pretentious restaurants, such as the one described in this essay, should be avoided.
   c. He prefers hot dogs from a sidewalk vendor to any food he could get from a fancy restaurant.
   d. Any meal can be enjoyable if one has the right dinner partner.

4. Which of the following from paragraph 10 is a metaphor?

   a. "...the plates were valuable parcels of land..."
   b. "...I have no idea which plate might be mine."
   c. "...a lamb chop tended to maintain its basic shape."
   d. "Apparently, though, that was too predictable."

5. Refer back to the use of the word "saffron" in paragraph 10. In the way that Sedaris uses it, saffron must refer to what aspect of the linguini?

   a. its smell
   b. its appearance
   c. its taste
   d. its warmth

Additional Questions for Writing and Discussion for Klockeman, "Vulgar Propriety"

OBJECTIVE *Analyze an essay.*	

1. What writing strategy does Klockeman use in paragraph 5?

   a. comparison
   b. cause and effect
   c. process
   d. definition

2. In paragraph 7, Klockeman uses several contrasting terms to compare settings and characters. Which of the following are NOT contrasting terms?

   a. opulent and minimalistic
   b. trapped and free
   c. accessorized and ornamented
   d. innocent and alluring

3. Klockeman's thesis statement refers to *Moulin Rouge* being "over the top." This cliché means the film

   a. was expensive to make.
   b. is extravagant.
   c. is difficult to watch.
   d. critically acclaimed.

4. "Vulgar Propriety" (the title of the essay) is an oxymoron, which is a figure of speech in which terms with contradictory meanings are used together. Considering this definition, which of the following is also an oxymoron?

   a. wind power
   b. new leaf
   c. romantic comedy
   d. jumbo shrimp

5. Klockeman's Web sources on her Works Consulted page all end with the date 5 Mar. 2009. This is the date that

   a. Klockeman wrote this paper.
   b. *Moulin Rouge* came out in theaters.
   c. Klockeman researched these sources.
   d. *Moulin Rouge* was released on DVD.

CHAPTER 9   Problem Solving

Activities to Support the Writing Assignment

OBJECTIVE 9.2 *Use collecting strategies to define a problem and develop solutions.*

1. List three problems that littering (or a topic of your choice) creates.

    1.

    2.

    3.

2. List three possible solutions to the problem of littering (or a topic of your choice).

    1.

    2.

    3.

3. Examples, statistics, and authority are used to provide evidence in a problem-solving essay. Imagine you are writing an essay on the problem of littering (or a topic of your choice). Answer these three questions:

1. Name one example of the problem.

2. What type of statistic could you include in your paper? (Remember, statistics mean numbers.)

3. Who would be an authority in your area who could give you information on the problem?

OBJECTIVE 9.3 *Shape your proposal.*

---

4. The thesis statement for a problem-solving essay always states the main problem and sometimes offers a broad solution. For example, this is a thesis statement for a paper on cheating on college campuses:

"Cheating has become a widespread problem on college campuses and can be stopped only by total commitment from both faculty and students to develop and adhere to a strict honor system."

Write a thesis statement for a problem-solving essay on the topic of littering (or a topic of your choice).

5. Identify a problem that is of local concern, perhaps in your community or on your college campus. Brainstorm on the topic. Include the effects of the problem, examples, and solutions.

Additional Questions for Writing and Discussion for Arum, "Your So-Called Education"

OBJECTIVE *Analyze an essay.*

1. Which of the following is NOT part of the author's story map, which lists three problems with undergraduate education?

   a. lack of rigor in coursework
   b. little effort put into coursework
   c. lack of improvement in writing and reasoning skills
   d. poor math instruction

2. Paragraph 9 begins the part of the essay that

   a. provides statistics to support the problem.
   b. discusses how financial aid affects the problem.
   c. suggests students should attend a community college before attending a four-year college.
   d. presents solutions to the problem.

3. According to the authors, which of the following should determine how resources and rewards for professors are distributed?

   a. student satisfaction
   b. financial standing
   c. student learning
   d. administrative decisions

4. Paragraph 8 uses the word "lassitude" to describe a student behavior. Given its context, what is the meaning of "lassitude"?

   a. mental weariness
   b. tendency to party
   c. attitudes toward professors
   d. misbehavior

5. Who is the primary audience for this essay?

   a. college students
   b. parents of college students
   c. college faculty
   d. college administrators

Additional Questions for Writing and Discussion for O'Shaughnessy, "But Can They Write?"

OBJECTIVE *Analyze an essay.*

1. What is the main problem O'Shaughnessy presents in this article?

    a. It is unwise for college students to major in history, political science, or philosophy.
    b. Business students often graduate from college expecting, but not getting, a high salary.
    c. The average class size for college business majors is too large.
    d. Spanish courses in college are more difficult than those in high school.

2. The evidence cited by O'Shaughnessy in the article comes from

    a. interviews.
    b. personal experience.
    c. surveys.
    d. research.

3. Often, problem-solving essays present a solution. In this article, the solution isn't stated directly but it is implied. This solution is to

    a. require business students to do more writing.
    b. have English professors teach some business courses.
    c. limit the number of students enrolled in business courses.
    d. reduce the number of students allowed to major in business.

4. What writing strategy does O'Shaughnessy use in paragraph 3?

    a. cause and effect
    b. comparison
    c. process
    d. definition

5. The term "slacker" in paragraph 1 is an example of

    a. jargon.
    b. a simile.
    c. slang.
    d. a cliché.

Additional Questions for Writing and Discussion for Surowiecki, "Debt By Degrees"

OBJECTIVE *Analyze an essay.*

---

1. What is the main problem presented in this essay?

   a. College tuition is too expensive.
   b. It is too easy for college students to borrow money.
   c. Debts for college students are too high.
   d. It is difficult for college graduates to find a job.

2. Which of the following is NOT a comparison made by the author in support of his thesis?

   a. comparing college students to homeowners
   b. comparing unemployment rates of college graduates and high school graduates
   c. comparing the economics of education to the economics of health care
   d. comparing manufacturing to education

3. One solution to the rising cost of college suggested by the author is to

   a. prevent students from over-borrowing.
   b. encourage students to pursue less expensive education, such as community college.
   c. pay teachers less.
   d. give incentives to businesses that do not require college-educated employees.

4. Paragraph 6 uses the term "exacerbated" in describing the Baumol problem. Which of the following is the best definition for "exacerbated"?

   a. irritated
   b. made violent
   c. made worse
   d. caused

5. What does the author include in his conclusion (paragraph 7)?

   a. recommendations with evidence
   b. recommendations alone
   c. recommendations with alternatives
   d. recommendations with specific examples

Additional Questions for Writing and Discussion for Leonhardt, "Even for Cashiers, College Pays Off"

OBJECTIVE *Analyze an essay.*

1. What is the main problem presented in this essay?

   a. the current idea that not everyone should go to college
   b. the high cost of college tuition
   c. the poor preparation of students for life after college
   d. the low percentage of students getting a four-year degree

2. For each argument against college education for the masses, the author

   a. provides a counterargument.
   b. provides evidence to support the argument.
   c. provides a chart to support his ideas.
   d. provides a personal anecdote that disproves the argument.

3. The writing strategy used in paragraph 12 is

   a. definition.
   b. cause and effect.
   c. process.
   d. comparison.

4. Paragraph 6 uses the word "panacea." In looking at its context, which of the following is the best definition of "panacea"?

   a. common practice
   b. solution to a problem
   c. suggestion
   d. problem

5. The author uses the first two paragraphs to

   a. present the opposing viewpoint.
   b. present the problem being discussed.
   c. compare today's educational systems in America and Europe.
   d. put the problem in a historical context.

Additional Questions for Writing and Discussion for Petsko, "An Open Letter to George M. Philip…"

OBJECTIVE *Analyze an essay.*

---

1. Which of the following is NOT one of the reasons Petsko cites for George M. Philip's decision to eliminate certain departments at SUNY Albany?

   a. Financial aid will not pay for these courses.
   b. The enrollment in the programs is down.
   c. Philip was forced to by the state legislature.
   d. Every college can't teach every subject.

2. Gregory Petsko is

   a. a student at SUNY.
   b. a chemistry professor at another college.
   c. a fellow professor at SUNY.
   d. a Classics professor at another university.

3. Which of the following structural patterns does Petsko use in his letter?

   a. He presents one problem at a time and follows it with a solution.
   b. He presents all the problems first and then goes on to discuss the solutions.
   c. He agrees with Philip's decisions and explains why he supports them.
   d. He uses a series of stories to support his thesis.

4. In paragraph 4, Petsko uses the phrase "eschewed your draconian…solution." Which of the following phrases would be an appropriate substitution for that phrase? Consult a dictionary if necessary.

   a. agreed with your logical solution
   b. questioned your unusual solution
   c. debated your controversial solution
   d. avoided using your excessively harsh solution

5. Which of the following is NOT a solution suggested by Petsko?

   a. make the courses mandatory
   b. involve the entire campus in the decision-making process
   c. have students take these courses from another college
   d. learn more about the content of the courses

Additional Questions for Writing and Discussion for Tannen, "The Argument Culture"

OBJECTIVE *Analyze an essay.*

1. Which of the following is a metaphor for argument that Tannen recommends we avoid?

    a. sports
    b. road rage
    c. society
    d. debate

2. What shaping strategy does Tannen use in paragraph 2 to support her point about the argument culture?

    a. definition
    b. classification
    c. comparison
    d. examples

3. What shaping strategy does Tannen use in paragraph 3 to describe public interactions?

    a. classification
    b. comparison
    c. definition
    d. process

4. Tannen uses the term "ubiquity" in paragraph 6. Re-read the paragraph. Using context clues, finish the following sentence. "Ubiquity" means that something is

    a. everywhere.
    b. misjudged.
    c. hard to find.
    d. doubtful.

5. Which one of the following is NOT a solution offered by Tannen?

    a. Change the culture to be less argumentative.
    b. Try another way beside argument to find the truth.
    c. Use metaphors that aren't combative.
    d. Write to the editor of the local paper.

Additional Questions for Writing and Discussion for Richman, "Can Citizen Journalism Pick Up the Pieces?"

> **OBJECTIVE** *Analyze an essay.*

1. According to Richman, the problem facing journalism today is

   a. the fact that citizen journalists aren't real journalists.
   b. that people are more interested in entertainment than news.
   c. that newspapers don't have enough money to stay in business.
   d. the eventual disappearance of print journalism.

2. What is Richman's primary solution to the problem discussed in his essay?

   a. more government funding for newspapers
   b. have news websites charge a fee for viewing articles
   c. combine several smaller papers into a larger newspaper
   d. the use of citizen journalists

3. In paragraph 3, Richman compares a functioning democracy to a chemical reaction equation. This type of figurative language is called

   a. a metaphor.
   b. irony.
   c. a simile.
   d. symbolism.

4. In paragraph 2, Richman uses the term "augment." Which of the following is an antonym (opposite) of "augment"?

   a. decrease
   b. improve
   c. change
   d. enlarge

5. March 28, 2009, is in each of the entries on Richman's Works Cited page. This is the date that

   a. Richman wrote his paper.
   b. Richman researched the information.
   c. each article was published.
   d. each article was entered into the college's database.

CHAPTER 10   Arguing

Activities to Support the Writing Assignment

OBJECTIVE 10.1 *Use techniques for developing a claim.*

1. Select a debatable topic about which you have a strong opinion. Take the topic and form it into a claim—a sentence that expresses your opinion of it. Avoid writing the sentence in first-person point of view. Then, list three logical reasons that support your opinion.

OBJECTIVE 10.5 *Use collecting strategies to develop an argument.*

2. With many argumentative topics, it is important to inform your reader regarding the history and present situation of the topic. Research the topic of legalizing gay marriage to find the following information:

1. any records of same-sex marriage from ancient history

2. Jack Baker and Michael McConnell's roles in the history of same sex marriage

3. the significance of September 21, 1996

4. the significance of November 6, 2012

OBJECTIVE 10.6 *Shape your argument.*

---

3. Select a campus, local, or state issue that is the subject of current debate. Explain two opposing viewpoints.

4. Here is a claim:

English should be made the official language of the United States.

List two reasons supporting this claim and two reasons opposing it.

5. Select a topic about which you want to write your argumentative essay. Write notes on the following:

1. Provide the information for your introductory paragraph: an interesting story, quote, statistic; background/history; and thesis statement.

2. List three logical reasons that support your thesis statement along with evidence.

3. Explain the opposing viewpoint.

4. Develop ideas for your concluding paragraph, which may include restating your main idea, predicting consequences, giving a powerful example, calling for action.

Additional Questions for Writing and Discussion for Cleaver, "The Internet: A Clear and Present Danger?"

OBJECTIVE *Analyze an essay.*

1. Which of the following suggests that this essay was originally written as a speech?

    a. the use of second-person point of view in the introduction
    b. the way the essay is divided by headings
    c. the way the essay is organized
    d. the fact that Cleaver presents her opinion, plus the opposition's

2. The argument in paragraph 17 appeals to

    a. reason.
    b. emotion.
    c. character.
    d. the opposition.

3. Which of the following is one of Cleaver's arguments against Internet restrictions?

    a. Restrictions will infringe on the rights guaranteed by the Constitution.
    b. Restrictions will slow down Internet technological development.
    c. Restrictions will be too difficult to enforce.
    d. Restrictions will change the way the Internet works.

4. The first paragraph of this essay uses the term "proprietary." In looking at the context of the word, "proprietary" deals with

    a. secrecy.
    b. expense.
    c. ownership.
    d. legality.

5. Which of the following is the thesis of Cleaver's argument?

    a. The Internet must be regulated in certain areas, especially when it comes to protecting children.
    b. There are both pros and cons when it comes to regulating the Internet.
    c. Parents must be more involved when it comes to regulating their children's activities on the Internet.
    d. The government must enact laws that protect children from pornography.

Additional Questions for Writing and Discussion for Manjoo, "You Have No Friends"

OBJECTIVE *Analyze an essay.*

1. Who is Manjoo's intended audience?

   a. people who use Facebook frequently
   b. people who have a Facebook page but don't use it much
   c. people who aren't on Facebook
   d. corporate officials at Facebook

2. Which of the following is NOT mentioned as a reason people don't use Facebook?

   a. Facebook takes too much work.
   b. Facebook makes it too easy to be in awkward situations.
   c. Facebook can create dangerous situations.
   d. Facebook makes it too easy for other people to know your business.

3. Which of the following does Manjoo NOT mention in his essay as a reason to use Facebook?

   a. Facebook is a tool to improve one's self-esteem.
   b. Facebook makes social connections easier.
   c. Knowing the details of your friends' lives makes you closer to them.
   d. Privacy controls let you be in charge of the information other people see.

4. Manjoo uses first-, second-, and third-person point of view throughout his paper. He uses second-person when he speaks directly to his reader, third-person when he describes people's objections to Facebook, and first-person

   a. in the introduction where he discusses Mark Zuckerberg, the founder of Facebook.
   b. in paragraph 2 when he addresses Facebook non-users.
   c. in paragraphs 10 and 11 when he describes Retelle's and Harris's viewpoints.
   d. in paragraph 5 when he describes his personal use of Facebook.

5. In paragraph 4, Manjoo compares the evolution of Facebook to the evolution of the mobile phone. This technique is known as

   a. an extended metaphor.
   b. a simile
   c. irony.
   d. symbolism.

Additional Questions for Writing and Discussion for Kliff, "And Why I Hate It…"

OBJECTIVE *Analyze an essay.*

1. The author argues that

    a. Facebook should limit the number of posts one can make.
    b. Facebook should automatically drop users who haven't been on the site for a certain period of time.
    c. Facebook is more important than what is happening in the "real world."
    d. much of the time spent on Facebook is wasted time.

2. In paragraph 3, Kliff discusses her "idiosyncrasies" that she posts on Facebook. "Idiosyncrasies" are

    a. things done by a large group of people.
    b. a person's distinctive behaviors.
    c. strange, almost bizarre behaviors.
    d. a special type of athletic ability.

3. Kliff uses the word "tenuous" to describe her Facebook friendships. The opposite (antonym) of "tenuous" is

    a. long-lasting.
    b. new.
    c. strong.
    d. fake.

4. According to Kliff, Facebook has gone from a website to help people connect with others to a place to

    a. look for jobs.
    b. be self-indulgent.
    c. post pictures.
    d. develop relationships.

5. Which of the following strategies of Rogerian argument does Kliff use in her essay?

    a. She is not confrontational.
    b. She offers a compromise or solution.
    c. She establishes common ground with the opposition.
    d. She empathizes with the opposition.

Additional Questions for Writing and Discussion for Holladay, "Cyberbullying"

> **OBJECTIVE** *Analyze an essay.*

1. What shaping strategy does Holladay use in paragraph 7?

    a. process
    b. cause and effect
    c. definition
    d. comparison

2. Re-read paragraph 15. Which of the following is a correct assumption regarding Formspring?

    a. It is more popular than Twitter among teenagers.
    b. It is not as well known as Facebook.
    c. It is easier to use than Facebook and Twitter.
    d. It is used primarily for cyberbullying.

3. The story of Phoebe Prince appeals to

    a. reason.
    b. character.
    c. emotion.
    d. ethics.

4. Paragraph 16 uses the term "ostensible." Using context clues, determine which of the following is the best definition of "ostensible."

    a. something that appears to be true
    b. something that is difficult to overcome
    c. something that is long-established
    d. something that is well-respected

5. The primary claim of this essay is a claim about

    a. fact and definition.
    b. cause and effect.
    c. value.
    d. solutions or policies.

Additional Questions for Writing and Discussion for Boyd and Marwick, "Bullying as True Drama"

OBJECTIVE *Analyze an essay.*

1. The essay discusses several anti-bullying efforts. The key point, however, is

    a. getting parents involved in what their children do online.
    b. how young people feel about themselves.
    c. making stronger anti-bullying laws.
    d. school administrators being aware of what is happening in their schools.

2. The story of Jamey Rodemeyer appeals to

    a. reason.
    b. character.
    c. emotion.
    d. ethics.

3. Paragraph 7 uses the term "innocuous" when describing teenage drama. Which of the following is a correct definition or synonym for "innocuous"?

    a. special
    b. harmless
    c. dangerous
    d. illegal

4. The primary claim in this essay is a claim about

    a. fact and definition.
    b. value.
    c. cause and effect.
    d. solutions or policies.

5. The concluding paragraph compares bullying in schools to bringing guns to school. This technique is known as

    a. a simile.
    b. irony.
    c. symbolism.
    d. an extended metaphor.

Additional Questions for Writing and Discussion for Helft, "Facebook Wrestles with Free Speech and Civility"

> **OBJECTIVE** *Analyze an essay.*

1. What is Dave Willner's job at Facebook?

   a. to work as a security guard
   b. to oversee legal matters
   c. to remove controversial content
   d. to design software

2. A "troll" is someone who

   a. creates fake profiles.
   b. bullies other Facebook users.
   c. hacks into Facebook.
   d. criticizes Facebook for its free speech policies.

3. In paragraph 2, Helft uses the prefix "quasi-" before "professional." This prefix changes the word professional to mean

   a. somewhat professional.
   b. extremely professional.
   c. not at all professional.
   d. exactly professional.

4. The opposing viewpoint of this article criticizes Facebook for

   a. violating First Amendment rights.
   b. allowing children to use Facebook.
   c. how it responds to problems.
   d. being too political.

5. Which type of appeal does Helft use in his article?

   a. appeal to reason
   b. appeal to character
   c. combined appeals
   d. appeal to emotion

Additional Questions for Writing and Discussion for Waters, "Why You Can't Cite Wikipedia in My Class"

1. Which of the following is NOT mentioned in the essay as one of the reasons Wikipedia is appealing?

    a. People are willing to contribute for free.
    b. It is very popular among college students.
    c. It gives people a place to publish in the fields they care about.
    d. It gives editors a place to practice their craft.

2. Which shaping strategy does Waters use in paragraphs 8 and 9?

    a. comparison
    b. process
    c. cause and effect
    d. definition

3. Paragraph 1 uses the term "aggregate" to describe labor. Considering the context in which the word is used, what is the meaning of "aggregate"?

    a. unpaid
    b. individual
    c. combined
    d. unskilled

4. Which of the following does Waters suggest as a possible solution to the problem presented in his essay?

    a. Colleges should block Wikipedia from campus computers.
    b. Users should have to pay a fee, thus making the website more credible.
    c. Only people with college degrees should be allowed to contribute to Wikipedia.
    d. Hold Wikipedia editors and contributors more accountable.

5. Which shaping strategy does Walters use in his conclusion?

    a. comparison
    b. examples
    c. definition
    d. cause and effect

Additional Questions for Writing and Discussion for Wilson, "Professors Should Embrace Wikipedia"

OBJECTIVE *Analyze an essay.*

1. According to the author, one of the reasons Wikipedia is popular among college students is

   a. it is free to use.
   b. the topics appeal to young people.
   c. it is easy to use.
   d. the hyperlinks in the articles are interesting to college students.

2. The author's thesis is that

   a. parts of Wikipedia should be off-limits to college students.
   b. college students should contribute to and edit Wikipedia.
   c. professors should work to improve Wikipedia, which would make it more suitable for college students to use.
   d. by charging a fee to use Wikipedia, the quality of the site would improve.

3. According to Wilson, what is perceived as the main problem with Wikipedia?

   a. too many people contributing to it
   b. advertisers having too much to say over the content
   c. it is too easy to use
   d. lack of academic authority

4. Which shaping strategy does the author use in paragraph 9?

   a. cause and effect
   b. comparison
   c. examples
   d. definition

5. Paragraph 6 uses the term "arcane." Which of the following would be an antonym (opposite) of "arcane"?

   a. mysterious
   b. unknown
   c. obscure
   d. popular

Additional Questions for Writing and Discussion for Carr, "Does the Internet Make You Dumber?"

OBJECTIVE *Analyze an essay.*

1. The main claim of this essay is a claim about

   a. fact or definition
   b. value
   c. cause and effect
   d. solutions or policies

2. Carr's thesis is that

   a. the Internet has both benefits and drawbacks.
   b. reading a book is far more beneficial than reading online.
   c. the Internet weakens one's ability to think deeply.
   d. multitaskers have higher brain function than people who do one thing at a time.

3. Which rhetorical appeal is used in paragraphs 5 through 9?

   a. pathos
   b. ethos
   c. logos
   d. combined appeals

4. Who is the primary audience for this essay?

   a. researchers
   b. frequent Internet users
   c. tech company owners
   d. parents

5. Which rhetorical appeal is used in paragraph 12?

   a. logos
   b. pathos
   c. ethos
   d. combined appeals

Additional Questions for Writing and Discussion for Sabatke, "Welfare Is Still Necessary for Women and Children in the U.S."

> **OBJECTIVE** *Analyze an essay.*

1. Sabatke says that her audience is white, conservative males. To which of the following groups would these men most likely belong?

   a. lawmakers
   b. professors
   c. social workers
   d. researchers

2. Throughout Sabatke's essay, there are numbers in parentheses. These numbers indicate

   a. volume numbers.
   b. dates.
   c. order of citations.
   d. page numbers.

3. Sabatke's essay map is

   a. part of the introductory paragraph.
   b. written in several sentences.
   c. found in paragraph 2.
   d. part of her thesis statement.

4. The most substantial change Sabatke made to her rough draft is

   a. more of her own opinion.
   b. more of the opposing viewpoint.
   c. interviews with women on welfare.
   d. inclusion of more research.

5. The primary debatable claim of this essay is a claim about

   a. cause and effect.
   b. fact or definition.
   c. value.
   d. a solution or policy.

CHAPTER 11   Responding to Literature

Activities to Support the Writing Assignment

> **OBJECTIVE 11.1** *Use techniques for responding to literature.*

1. Read the lines from "The Road Not Taken," a poem by Robert Frost, in Chapter 11. Then go to YouTube and watch Nickelback's video "If Today Was Your Last Day," which shows the lyrics on the screen. Take notes on the similarities between the song and the poem regarding word choice and meaning.

2. Read "The Story of an Hour" in Chapter 11 of your text. On the Internet, find the poem "Aunt Jennifer's Tigers" by Adrienne Rich. How is the Mallards' marriage similar to the marriage of the aunt and uncle in Rich's poem?

3. Create a timeline for Toni Cade Bambara's "The Lesson" in Chapter 11 of your text.

4. Analyze the point of view of "The Story of an Hour" in Chapter 11 by doing the following activities:

   1. Explain what point of view the story is written in and how you know that.

2. Rewrite paragraph 13 in first person point of view.

3. How would the story be different if it had been written in first person from Mrs. Mallard's point of view?

5. Re-read "Miracle Workers" by Taylor Mali in Chapter 11 of your text. Take notes specifically on anything he says about teachers. What do you find surprising, humorous, or expected? Given that Mali has experience teaching middle school, high school, and college, do parts of his poem seem more applicable to a certain age group than others? Explain.

Additional Questions for Writing and Discussion for Bambara, "The Lesson"

1. In what point of view is this story written?

    a. third-person omniscient
    b. selective omniscient
    c. first person
    d. stream-of-consciousness

2. What lesson is Miss Moore trying to teach the children?

    a. White people are crazy.
    b. They need to learn to accept their place in society.
    c. Blacks and whites will never be equal.
    d. Everyone should have an equal chance at happiness.

3. Who is the main character of this story?

    a. Miss Moore
    b. Sugar
    c. Mercedes
    d. Sylvia

4. The last line of the story, "But ain't nobody gonna beat me at nuthin," represents not only the race between Sylvia and Sugar but also Sylvia's attitude about the lesson she learned that day. This type of literary device is known as

    a. symbolism.
    b. irony.
    c. tone.
    d. metaphor.

5. The author uses incorrect grammar and spelling throughout the story, along with profanity in a few places. She chose this type of writing style because she

    a. wrote the story when she was a child, before she was educated.
    b. wanted to contrast the language differences between the black characters and white characters.
    c. wanted the reader to have a negative attitude toward Sylvia.
    d. wanted to give a realistic portrayal of the characters.

Additional Questions for Writing and Discussion for Five Contemporary Poems

---

OBJECTIVE *Analyze an essay.*

---

1. In "Child of the Americas" Morales uses a metaphor to compare the English language with

    a. hand gestures.
    b. the ghettos of New York.
    c. the blade of a knife.
    d. other languages.

2. In the first stanza of "Miracle Workers," Mali uses a simile to compare

    a. sleep to teaching.
    b. sleep to music.
    c. teachers to students.
    d. Sunday nights to weeknights.

3. In "Perhaps the World Ends Here," Harjo uses personification as a very effective figure of speech. Which of the following is an example of personification?

    a. "We chase chickens or dogs away from it."
    b. "This table has been a house in the rain…"
    c. "We pray of suffering and remorse."
    d. "Our dreams drink coffee with us…"

4. In "Facing It," Komunyakaa writes, "I'm a window." This an example of

    a. a simile.
    b. personification.
    c. a metaphor.
    d. diction.

5. The last stanza of "End and Beginning" speaks of "somebody" who "must recline…" in the grass, "a stalk of rye in the teeth, ogling the clouds." Given the context of the poem, whom does this passage describe?

    a. the townspeople who are cleaning up after the war
    b. the soldiers who didn't die
    c. the future generation
    d. the war dead

Additional Questions for Writing and Discussion for Rexroth: "Facing It: Reflection on War"

OBJECTIVE *Analyze an essay.*

1. According to Rexroth, images such as "letters like smoke" symbolize

    a. ghosts.
    b. fire.
    c. death.
    d. the wall.

2. Paragraph 5 of Rexroth's essay uses the term "juxtaposition." If two things are juxtaposed they are

    a. opposite.
    b. close together.
    c. large in size.
    d. far away from each other.

3. The thesis of Rexroth's essay focuses on the poem's

    a. setting.
    b. themes.
    c. characters.
    d. sound.

4. According to Rexroth, the word "facing" has two meanings. The speaker is standing face-to-face with the wall, but he is also facing his memories of the war. This type of dual meaning is known as

    a. simile and metaphor.
    b. tone and style.
    c. literal and figurative.
    d. rhyme and rhythm.

5. In paragraph 7, Rexroth refers to the line in the poem where Komunyakaa describes the white veteran who has "lost his right arm inside the stone." Rexroth goes on to state that this could have two meanings. One is that the man actually lost an arm during the war. The other meaning is

    a. the angle at which the man is standing distorts the image.
    b. the man feels helpless and incomplete.
    c. the man is holding something that hides his arm.
    d. the man is a ghostly image.

Additional Questions for Writing and Discussion for Russell: "Death: The Final Freedom"

OBJECTIVE *Analyze an essay.*

1. What is the thesis of Russell's essay?

   a. People in an unhappy marriage should work to keep the marriage together.
   b. "The Story of an Hour" should be viewed as more than just feminist literature.
   c. It is much easier for a woman to get a divorce today than it was during the time the story was set.
   d. People have only themselves to blame for their unhappiness.

2. In paragraph 3, Russell puts the word "died" in quotation marks. Why did he do this?

   a. because he is quoting directly from the story
   b. because the character in the story didn't actually die
   c. because he wants to stress the importance of the word
   d. because he is saying that being in an unhappy marriage is worse than death

3. The first part of paragraph 2 puts the story in a

   a. historical context.
   b. social context.
   c. literary context.
   d. modern context.

4. In paragraph 13 of "The Story of an Hour," Mrs. Mallard describes her husband as having "kind, tender hands." If Russell had used that quote in his essay, where would be the best place for it?

   a. at the end of paragraph 2
   b. in the conclusion
   c. in the middle of paragraph 3
   d. in the introduction

5. Which of the following is the primary shaping strategy used by Russell?

   a. investigating changes in interpretation
   b. arguing
   c. evaluating
   d. explaining relationships

CHAPTER 12   Researching

Activities to Support the Writing Assignment

OBJECTIVE 12.1 *Keep purpose and audience in mind when developing a research topic.*

1. Select three topics that would be suitable for a researched essay. Consider the areas of career, medicine, and social issues. Write a sentence explaining your approach to each topic.

   1.

   2.

   3.

2. Select one topic you feel is suitable for a researched essay. Explain the purpose and audience for this researched essay.

   Purpose:

   Audience:

3. Make notes for your research essay proposal. Include your purpose and audience, along with a description of the resources and time necessary to complete this project.

4. Using your college library's database, find three possible sources for your researched essay. Prepare bibliographic notes of those three sources, using MLA format.

5. Write a working thesis for your research essay.

CHAPTER 13   Researched Writing

Activities to Support the Writing Assignment

> **OBJECTIVE 13.1** *Use techniques for writing a working thesis statement.*

1. Using the research topic you selected in Chapter 12, or another topic approved by your instructor, begin working on your thesis.

    1. Draft a working thesis.

    Then answer these questions:

    1. What is my purpose for writing?

    2. Based on my purpose, do I need to adjust my working thesis? If so, rewrite the thesis.

OBJECTIVE 13.3 *Use sources to support your claims.*

2. Continue to gather sources for your researched essay. In addition to any sources you may have gotten from your library's databases, broaden your list of sources. Consider primary sources, such as interviews and questionnaires. Make a list of at least three additional sources.

OBJECTIVE 13.6 *Shape your research essay.*

3. Develop a working outline for your researched essay, using the model found in Chapter 13.

4. Develop an introductory paragraph for your researched essay. Consider what your audience needs to know: Do any terms need to be defined? Is the history of your topic relevant to your thesis?

5. Practice using and documenting sources by adding a direct quotation to your introduction. Using MLA format, write your in-text citation and the Works Cited list entry.

Appendix A

Academic Success

Now You're Thinking • Information Literacy • Time Management • Power Up for Online Learning • Good Notes Are Your Best Study Tool • Prepare for Test Success

Now You're Thinking

HOW DO YOU GET FROM HERE TO THERE?

THINK ABOUT IT

Good thinking skills will differentiate you from other job candidates and will give you a competitive advantage. Step into the job and perform with confidence. Stop and think. Identify the real issue. Know when information is critical and when it's not. Explore alternatives. Decide. Make it happen. Be successful.

> " *Know your strengths and grow with your strengths.* "

Critical Thinking *is the #1 skill of increasing importance in today's workplace. What are you doing to develop this skill?*

10 QUESTIONS TO GUIDE YOUR NEXT BIG DECISION

1. What is going on?
2. What am I trying to accomplish?
3. Do I need more information?
4. What assumptions am I making?
5. Is this information accurate?
6. Am I being objective?
7. What else is missing?
8. What are the alternatives?
9. What resources do I need?
10. How will I communicate my decision?

5 STEPS TO BETTER THINKING

1. **STOP AND THINK**
   Think before you react.

2. **RECOGNIZE ASSUMPTIONS**
   Separate fact from opinion.

3. **EVALUATE INFORMATION**
   Efficiently evaluate information and suspend judgment.

4. **DRAW CONCLUSIONS**
   Decide what to do.

5. **PLAN OF ACTION**
   Implement your decision.

Keys to CRITICAL THINKING

- **R** Stop and Think
- **R** ecognize Assumptions
- **E** valuate Information
- **D** raw Conclusions
- Plan of Action

WHAT IS YOUR THINKING STYLE?

You have a preferred thinking style that drives how you approach problems and make decisions. Understand your personal thinking style and learn to use it to build your strengths. Be prepared so you can describe your strengths to potential employers.

To learn more about your personal thinking style, go to **www.ThinkWatson.com** and take the Critical Thinking Challenge.

 SEVEN POSITIVE STYLES

Take the Assessment and Learn Your Strengths:

1. **ANALYTICAL:** planful, orderly, methodical
2. **INQUISITIVE:** curious, alert, interested in the surrounding world
3. **INSIGHTFUL:** prudent, humble, reflective
4. **OPEN-MINDED:** empathic, tolerant of others, fair-minded
5. **SYSTEMATIC:** strategic, process-oriented, sees big-picture
6. **TIMELY:** efficient, reliable, resourceful
7. **TRUTH-SEEKING:** independent, tough-minded, skeptical

ALWAYS LEARNING   **PEARSON**

Information Literacy

Is Essential to Success

> " Drowning in data overload? Information literacy will help you stay afloat. "

Are You INFORMATION LITERATE?

WHAT IT IS *Information literacy* has several components:

- ▶ The ability to search for and access information
- ▶ The ability to understand and evaluate information
- ▶ The ability to choose and apply the information most useful in a given situation

WHY YOU NEED IT Our world is characterized by information overload. Not only is there more information in general, but also the rapid growth of technology has created:

- ▶ more sources of information
- ▶ more ways to access information
- ▶ more jobs focused on information

INFORMATION LITERACY *step by step*

step ① **Search for and Access Information.** Online information is extensive and accessible, but your library also has much to offer (books and resource materials, periodicals, online academic databases, staff who can help you navigate). Look for a tutorial—online or in person at your library—on what to use and how to use it.

step ② **Understand Information.** In such a fast-paced world, it can be hard to take your time. Slow down and make sure you understand what you are reading.

step ③ **Evaluate Information.** This skill is especially crucial with online materials, because information on the Internet is not necessarily screened or approved. Ask these questions:

- ▶ What organization published this? Is it reliable, reputable, objective?
- ▶ Who wrote this, and with what intent? Does the author have respectable credentials?
- ▶ Is this material fact or opinion—or both? Does it have a bias or particular perspective?
- ▶ Is this material current enough for my purposes?
- ▶ Are claims backed up with solid evidence?

step ④ **Choose the Best Information.** Even after you have narrowed down your materials to information that is reliable and high quality, you are likely to still have far too much information. Think critically to choose what will serve your particular goal.

step ⑤ **Use Information.** Put the information you have obtained to work *effectively* (as support for your thesis in a writing project, as visual evidence for a class presentation, as key points in a debate) and *ethically* (with proper source citations).

STAY SAFE, STAY LEGAL

In this "information age," technology has raised new issues of ethics, legality, and safety. Keep these guidelines in mind:

- ▶ **Protect Yourself.** You will have usernames and passwords for technological devices, information sources, social networking tools, and more. Read privacy guidelines and choose settings that protect you. Keep usernames and passwords to yourself.

- ▶ **Respect Intellectual Property.** Copying anyone's material and passing it off as your own work is plagiarism. Internet and computer technology makes it easy to cut and paste. Make sure that you correctly cite and provide source notes for any information you use word for word.

- ▶ **Follow the Rules.** Certain sources charge access fees. Don't share what you've paid for—or use what someone else has paid for—if it is against the rules. Copyright law says that you cannot legally copy or share certain documents, images, or audio files.

- ▶ **Know Institutional Policies.** Read and follow your institution's policy on how to access and use information sources. Remember that your institution's library pays fees for many academic databases so that students can use them free of charge. Ask a librarian for help when you are confused about a policy or need to access information from an academic database.

GET **TECH** SAVVY*!*

With so much information accessible primarily—or even only—through a computer, information literacy requires at least a basic level of technological prowess.

KNOW HOW TO USE THE COMPUTER(S) AVAILABLE TO YOU. To improve skills, use a manual, an online tutorial, or a real-time tutor. Contact your help desk or IT services for support.

NAVIGATE YOUR COURSE MANAGEMENT SYSTEM (CMS). Whether your institution uses BlackBoard, Moodle, or another CMS, learn how it functions so that you can use it for your courses.

GET COMFORTABLE WITH SPECIFIC SOFTWARE. Information that you locate may require that you be able to use programs such as Word, PowerPoint, Photoshop, or Pages.

UNDERSTAND THE BASICS OF INTERNET SEARCHING. Know how to use reliable search engines such as Google or Yahoo.

HANG ON TO INFORMATION THAT YOU FIND USEFUL. Be able to save information in various ways such as:

- ▶ Bookmarking a website so you can return to it
- ▶ Downloading a file onto your computer or flash drive
- ▶ Copying and pasting material into a document (noting source, author, and URL)

ALWAYS LEARNING

PEARSON

What's the Value of Time Management?

> **"Everyone begins with the same 24 hours in the day. How you use it is up to you."**

PLANNING YOUR TIME

There are 168 hours in a week. How many go toward the basic time demands of school?

STUDY TIME RULE OF THUMB For every hour in class, expect to study 2 to 3 hours outside of class.

Example:
15 hours of class a week × 2½ hours/class = 37½ hours of studying

Academic time commitment per week: 15 (class hours) + 37½ (study hours) = 52½ hours

SLEEP TIME Although students average less sleep, research shows that getting at least 7–8 hours of sleep each night boosts your ability to learn and remember.

Ideal time for sleep/week = 49–56 hours.

WHAT'S LEFT? For this example of a student with a 15-hour course load, about 60 hours per week. But if you work, subtract that time, too.

Example: 60 hours – Work 25 hours = 35 hours left for everything else (eating, commuting, errands, social time, down time).

Ask: *Do I have enough time to take care of my personal needs?*

WHERE DOES YOUR TIME GO?
To see how you use your time, track it for one week. (See **www.MyStudentSuccessLab.com** — Time Management Topic has a sample Time Log in MS Excel.)

	Mon	Tues	Wed	Thurs	Fri	Sat	Sun
6:00 a.m.							
7:00 a.m.							
8:00 a.m.							
9:00 a.m.							

PLANNING

START BIG: Plan for the term. Write important due dates, exams, and commitments on your calendar. Adjust schedules for crunch times.

PLAN BACKWARDS: Working back from assignment due dates and test dates, plan how much time you'll need to prepare—then schedule it.

KEEP PLANNING: Set aside time to plan your week, each week. Then, adjust plans daily.

ASK: *Do my plans support my biggest goals?*

PRIORITIZING

Focusing on important goals helps you decide what to do when you can't get everything done.

CREATE to-do lists of everything that needs to get done.

REVIEW lists daily. What helps you meet your goals?

PRIORITIZE the most important items. Do them first. Let less important ones wait.

all about PROCRASTINATION

► **Procrastination:** The act of putting off important tasks, often in favor of easier, low-priority ones. Not a synonym for *laziness*. Procrastination is common, but can cause serious problems.

COMMON REASONS
1. Feeling paralyzed by a big project
2. Wanting your work to be perfect
3. Fear of failure
4. Habit ("I've put things off before and done fine")
5. Thinking that you work best under pressure

COSTS Incomplete or low-quality work, stress, loss of sleep, lower self-esteem, broken commitments, not being trusted when working with others.

SOLUTIONS
1. Just start. Right now. Even a little.
2. Create a plan that breaks the project into small, manageable steps with due dates for each step. Then work step by step.
3. Ask: *What's blocking me from starting?* Identifying the block can help you move past it.
4. Experiment: If you think you thrive under pressure, set a fake early deadline.
5. Get a study partner to check on your progress.
6. Write a pro and con list of procrastinating on your project.

The Art of Saying "No"

If you consistently feel overwhelmed, learn to say "no" to extra projects, commitments, even family and friends. Mean what you say. "No" doesn't mean "*maybe.*"

ORGANIZE TO SAVE TIME AND STAY ON TRACK

FIND A CALENDARING SYSTEM THAT WORKS FOR YOU
Is it a Google, iCal, or Microsoft Outlook calendar; a smartphone; or a printed planner? Choose what works for you and use it consistently.

ORGANIZE YOUR STUDY SPACE
Rate yourself and take action as needed to improve.

	Never				Always
I have quick and easy access to my study supplies.	1	2	3	4	5
I have all my course materials organized.	1	2	3	4	5
I have one location where I can read, take notes, and/or work on a computer.	1	2	3	4	5
My study space is free of distractions.	1	2	3	4	5

ALWAYS LEARNING   **PEARSON**

Power up for *Online Course* Success

Online courses offer flexibility so you can learn in your own environment on your own time. Here are some tips and techniques to help you succeed in all your online courses.

MYTHS and FACTS about Online Education

MYTHS	FACTS
▶ Online courses are less rigorous than on-ground courses.	▶ **Not necessarily.** Usually, you will be expected to do more writing and participate more actively in discussions compared to a traditional classroom.
▶ You'll have less personal contact with an online instructor.	▶ **It depends.** You may find it is easier to initiate contact in the online environment. Many online instructors are extremely responsive to student contact although the majority of contact is through writing, not face-to-face.
▶ Online education is lower quality.	▶ **Not so.** Online courses have to meet the same accreditation standards that traditional schools do, and often use the same instructors and curriculum as their traditional counterparts.

BOTTOM LINE: The online classroom is what you make of it.

Know Your MOST PRODUCTIVE STUDY TIMES

One of the most positive factors in online learning may be just this: the ability to focus your studies during your peak times. Pay attention to discover when those times occur. That way, you can login to class and study during your peak times, not your valley times.

Ask: When am I most and least productive?

- Are you an owl (highly alert and productive at night)?
- Are you a lark (most productive early in the day)?
- Are you a person whose peak times vary over the course of the day?
- Do your peak times vary during the week vs. the weekend?

STUDY SPACE

A personalized work space allows you to be more efficient. Try to set up a dedicated study space for doing your class work in the way that is best for you, where you are comfortable both mentally and physically. Keep these factors in mind:

- lighting and outlets
- noise and potential for interruption
- seating that allows for good posture
- availability of course materials

Final Tip: Avoid creating your ideal study space in a place you will need to vacate later.

STAY ORGANIZED

Maintain your online success by keeping your class work and resources in order:

- ▶ Name documents and files logically, so they will be easier to reference when they are not as fresh in your mind.
- ▶ Maintain organized online files to make searches easier.
- ▶ Decide which course texts you will keep for later reference, and place them in a central location.
- ▶ Regularly back up your work!

Guidelines for Giving Feedback Online

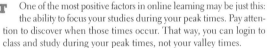
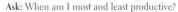

1. Be clear and succinct about what you want to say.
2. Emphasize the positive aspects of the feedback in the opening of your message, and always end the message with a positive and motivating tone. In the body of the message, provide the feedback and any constructive criticism you think is necessary.
3. Be descriptive in your feedback, rather than evaluative or judgmental.
4. Do not make any generalizations or assumptions when giving feedback, so avoid words like *all*, *never*, *always*, *everyone*, *only*, and *you*.
5. Limit your advice on how to fix the work. Often the most useful feedback is helping the person to recognize or better understand the area(s) that need improvement.

Guidelines for Receiving Feedback Online

1. Separate yourself from your emotions and try just to hear the comments. Do not make excuses or evaluate whether it is right or wrong. Just listen.
2. Look for the practical advice within the feedback. Pick out the constructive part of the message that you need to keep in mind for the future.
3. If the feedback was mostly criticism without any constructive advice and you do not know how to address the issue, go back to the person who gave it. Try to discover what steps you might reasonably take to make an improvement.
4. Try to see the big picture. Have you gotten feedback with similar comments before? Are there common areas that people always bring up? Clue in, and realize that if you are hearing the same feedback often or from multiple sources, it may be accurate. Do something about it.
5. Realize that people who give you feedback often have your best interests at heart.

Be SMART in Setting Goals

When setting a goal, know what you're aiming for and why. Write down your long-term goals to stay motivated. Then, break your long-term goals into smaller steps that move you closer to your target. When writing your long- or short-term goals, follow the SMART model:

S = Specific
M = Measurable
A = Attainable
R = Realistic
T = Timely

GOAL SETTING
S PECIFIC
M EASURABLE
A TTAINABLE
R EALISTIC
T IMELY

ALWAYS LEARNING

PEARSON

Get Things Done with Virtual Teams

A NEW WAY TO LINK TO A TEAM

Technology hasn't changed the fact that success demands teamwork. However, it has changed the way that team members *connect*— electronically instead of in person—and that changes the game. Where do you find virtual teams?

VIRTUAL COLLEGE As a college student, you are on teams with your instructors, fellow students, and advisors. With online courses, most or all interactions will be virtual. Many traditional courses have some online component such as a course site on which you can post comments, e-mail your instructor, and submit work.

> " *The key to virtual team success is communication.* "

VIRTUAL WORKPLACE As an employee, you are on teams with co-workers and supervisors. Because working remotely saves time and money, more work teams are virtual. You will need to communicate and collaborate with teammates in different locations and time zones. Some virual teamwork tools:

▶ Skype (video chat with screen sharing ability)
▶ Campfirenow.com (group chat room that stores transcripts of meetings)
▶ Google docs (document collaboration tool)

SOCIAL NETWORKING With tools like Facebook or Google Groups, you can create a virtual team focused on any goal you choose—raising money for a cause, for example, or getting involved in politics in your neighborhood.

SUCCESS IN THE VIRTUAL WORKPLACE

Many of the strategies that help you in the virtual classroom carry over into the virtual workplace.

KNOW THE TECHNOLOGY. Ask your supervisor what technology you need to use to do your job. Then get trained on it. Companies usually offer training in the collaborative technologies they use to help their employees communicate and share materials.

STAY ON TOP OF TASKS. Just because no one can look over your cubicle wall doesn't mean you are any less accountable for achieving work goals. Set a schedule of tasks and stick to it.

FIND FACE TIME. No matter how easy it is to communicate virtually, face-to-face meetings are necessary from time to time. Occasional in-person meetings can help a team grow relationships, work through conflicts, and build positive energy together.

Keeping It Friendly Online

When you communicate through writing, you miss out on the information transmitted through tone of voice, facial expression, and body language. Here are some tips for staying civil with co-workers and classmates:

▶ Read over your comments/posts/blog entries before you hit "send." Make sure they don't sound rude, insulting, or harsh.
▶ Avoid all caps (IT READS LIKE YOU ARE SHOUTING).
▶ Use polite language liberally. *Please, thank you, appreciate,* and other respectful words and phrases go a long way.
▶ When it looks like e-mails are not getting the point across, pick up the phone and talk in real time.
▶ If you can, video chat using a program like Skype when you need a closer approximation to an in-person conversation.

SUCCESS IN THE VIRTUAL CLASSROOM

How can you work toward your goals in an online learning environment?

LEARN THE LMS. Your first task is to get up to speed on the LMS (learning management system) your course uses, as well as any other technologies you need to use to share documents or interact with classmates.

MANAGE YOURSELF. Self-motivation and discipline are crucial to online course success. Read your syllabus to understand course expectations. Set goals for yourself and pursue them step by step.

SET UP A SCHEDULE. Put important dates in your calendar—assignments due, quizzes and tests, online "meetings." If tasks don't have specific due dates, assign dates on your own.

COMMUNICATE WITH FELLOW STUDENTS. When you connect with the other students in the course, you build relationships that will make it easier to work together on projects or papers. Post questions, respond to comments, and share interesting videos or articles.

TEAMWORK TIPS

General teamwork strategies apply to any interaction, whether in-person or virtual.

▶ Set goals as a team.
▶ Get clear on your responsibilities.
▶ Do what you say you will do—on time.
▶ Ask questions when you are confused.
▶ Stay open-minded when considering ideas from others.
▶ Value diversity and avoid prejudice.

ALWAYS LEARNING

PEARSON

Prepare for Test Success

PREPARE OVER TIME

1. Your primary goal in any course: To *learn the material.*
2. The goal of any test: To *measure what you have learned.*
3. Conclusion: *If you are learning, you are preparing effectively for tests.*

Here's how to keep your focus on learning so that passing tests is a step along the way to learning rather than your top goal.

KEEP UP WITH READINGS AND ASSIGNMENTS. Try to read assigned materials ahead of the class time when they will be discussed. Stay on top of homework, writing assignments, and projects.

PUT YOUR NOTES TO USE. Your notes are a great study tool—if you look at them. Set a schedule for reading your notes. Review them within a couple of hours of class if you can, or maybe once a week at a designated time.

SCHEDULE AHEAD. First, at the beginning of your course, put all test and quiz dates into your calendar—for all classes you are taking. This allows you to see your responsibilities at a glance and plan ahead for crunch times. Second, build study time into your schedule before important tests, midterms, or finals.

SPREAD OUT YOUR STUDYING. Cramming (studying intensely the night before a test) often results in temporary learning. To learn material so that it stays with you—and so that you can use it in other courses and in the workplace—study on a regular basis.

COMBAT TEST ANXIETY

A moderate level of stress can actually boost test performance. However, too much can lead to test anxiety—a high level of stress that can affect your concentration, create physical symptoms (nausea, headaches), and cause you to forget what you've learned. What can you do?

- **Prepare effectively.** Preparation is your first line of defense. When you know the material, you will be more confident that you can show that knowledge on a test.
- **Get help.** You'll work in pairs and teams at almost any job—why go it alone at school? Ask for help from your instructor, a tutor, a fellow student.
- **Be realistic.** The test is a chance to show what you've learned, not a measure of your value as a person.
- **Focus on your goal.** Remind yourself of the long-term goal that your success in this course will help you reach, and see the test as just one step along the path.

Test Day Tips

KEEP AN EYE ON THE TIME. Know how much time you have and plan out a rough idea of how you will use it.

DO EASY QUESTIONS FIRST. Scan the test, answer what comes easiest to you, and then spend the bulk of the time on questions that challenge you.

WORK INDEPENDENTLY. Cheating undermines your goal to learn and use what you've learned.

STAY CALM. Bring a special object or wear a certain clothing item if it calms you, and remember to breathe.

MAKE A FACT SHEET. Before you start, write down formulas, definitions, or other information that you don't want to forget.

READ QUESTIONS CAREFULLY. Avoid mistakes that come from misreading a test question.

TACKLING DIFFERENT TYPES OF TESTS

- For *objective tests* (multiple-choice, true/false, fill-in-the-blank, matching questions), keep an eye out for *qualifiers* like "always" or "sometimes" that affect the meaning of a question.
- For *essay tests*, read questions carefully and take a few minutes to plan out your response before you begin to write.
- For *open book tests*, don't assume you'll have an easy time. Access to the materials means you will need to demonstrate more in-depth thinking.
- For *online tests*, set up before you start—know how much time you have (and note if there is an onscreen clock), gather and open any materials you are permitted to use, and eliminate potential distractions or interruptions.

Appendix B
Life Skills

Set and Achieve Your Goals • Stay Well and Manage Stress • Succeeding in Your Diverse World • Get Things Done with Virtual Teams • Civility Paves the Way to Success • Maintaining Your Financial Sanity • Protect Your Personal Data • Strategies and Tactics for Military Students

Set and Achieve Your Goals

GOALS ARE EVERYWHERE

Setting and working toward goals will help you make the most of your potential in every aspect of your life:

- School (grades, major, length of time in school, graduation)
- Workplace (jobs, advancement, earnings)
- Wellness (exercise, eating right, maintaining a healthy weight, getting sleep)
- Finances (saving more, controlling spending, managing earnings)
- Relationships (family, friends, coworkers)
- Technology (controlling technology use, developing technology skills)
- Personal development (knowledge, spirituality, vision)

MAKE YOUR GOALS S.M.A.R.T.

If you design a goal according to the S.M.A.R.T. criteria, you stand a better chance of achieving it.

SPECIFIC. Be as *specific* as you can. You may not know where to start if your goal is "do well in school this term," but you can certainly get focused on "earn at least a B in accounting."

MEASURABLE. Design your goal so that you can *measure* your progress. If you want that B, for example, you can look at every assignment and test grade you get over the term to see if you are moving in the right direction.

ACHIEVABLE. Make sure you have the ability and the motivation to work toward the goal you set. If your goal is way out of your reach, you will set yourself up for failure. If it is *achievable*, you are more likely to follow through.

REALISTIC. Set goals that are *realistic* for you, given your circumstances. For a student working full time, for example, it may not be realistic to take a full course load.

TIME FRAME. Connect your goal to a specific *time frame*. Due dates are motivators. Decide that you will get your credit card debt paid off by the end of the calendar year, for example.

SHORT-TERM AND LONG-TERM GOALS

No one achieves a long-term goal in one jump. Short-term goals are stepping stones leading to your biggest long-term goals.

SHORT-TERM GOALS
A *short-term goal* happens over hours, days, weeks, or at the most several months. Because it's easier to focus on these smaller, more defined goals, it helps to break long-term goals down into steps consisting of one short-term goal after another. Putting away $100 each month, for example, is a set of short-term goals leading to a long-term goal of making a down payment on a home.

LONG-TERM GOALS
A *long-term goal* is achieved over six months, a year, five years, or even longer. Examples include working toward a particular GPA over a year's time, earning a degree or certificate, training for a 10K race, or saving for that down payment.

LONGEST-TERM GOALS
Step way back and think about your *personal mission*. What do you want to be, do, achieve over the course of your life? These are your longest-term goals and they can provide a context for all other goals you pursue.

GET PERSONAL

The more meaningful a goal is to you, the more likely you are to reach it—and to be glad you made the effort. Start any goal-setting process by looking carefully at what is important to you.

DREAMS What have you always dreamed of having, doing, becoming? Let your dreams percolate and help you determine your long-term life goals.

VALUES When you are pursuing a goal, it is often challenging to stick with it. If the goal is based on something that you value, you are more likely to hang in there when the going gets tough.

ABILITIES AND INTERESTS What do you do well? What do you like to do? Having ability and interest will make a challenging goal-achievement process that much easier—and maybe even fun.

CIRCUMSTANCES Your circumstances affect the goals you need to achieve. For example, parents need to care for children; students living independently need to earn money to pay for expenses; students with learning disabilities need to make time for additional academic support.

Stay Well *and* Manage Stress

> **"** *Stress is a reality for everyone. Good health helps you manage it.* **"**

ALL ABOUT STRESS

Start with some important facts about **stress**:

1. Stress is an unavoidable fact of life.
2. Both positive *and* negative experiences can cause stress.
3. Stress can be helpful or harmful, depending on the amount and the circumstances.
4. Wellness helps you minimize and manage stress.

HOW CAN STRESS HELP? Studies have shown that moderate levels of stress can motivate. Consider three students' experiences:

▶ **Student 1**, completely unprepared and paralyzed by stress, could not stay calm on test day. Result: A low grade.

▶ **Student 2**, feeling a moderate level of stress, studied hard to feel more confident about the test. Result: A good grade.

▶ **Student 3**, supremely confident, had no stress and therefore felt no need to study. Result: A low grade (a big surprise to Student 3).

MENTAL WELLNESS

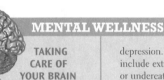

TAKING CARE OF YOUR BRAIN

Your brain is an essential organ. How can you keep it healthy so that it functions well?

▶ **Strive for balance.** Too much time working OR playing can lead to stress. Try to balance the energy you put toward coursework, job, family, and friends.

▶ **Find your "self-soothers."** Do you like music? Rock climbing? Video games? Knitting? Figure out what calms you and make it a regular part of your life.

▶ **Connect.** Spend time with people you care about. Combine responsibilities with social time—study with a friend, exercise with your child.

MENTAL HEALTH PROBLEMS

The following illnesses are treatable. A professional at the student health center or counseling center can help students find the right combination of therapy, lifestyle changes, and/or medication.

▶ **Depression.** When sad feelings last too long or seem overwhelming, they can signal depression. Symptoms also include extreme fatigue, over- or undereating, and feeling worthless.

▶ **Eating disorders.** These include:
—Anorexia nervosa (severe restriction of eating)
—Bulimia nervosa (bingeing and then purging)
—Binge eating disorder (bingeing without the purging, often with weight gain)

▶ **Anxiety disorders.** These include:
—Generalized anxiety disorder (chronic anxiety and excessive worry)
—Obsessive-Compulsive Disorder, or OCD (inability to calm obsessions and compulsions)
—Post-Traumatic Stress Disorder, or PTSD (persistent disturbing thoughts following a frightening event)

GET PHYSICAL

EAT RIGHT Food is fuel. You would not overfill your gas tank or put in Gatorade instead of gasoline—give your body the same respect. Follow these basics:

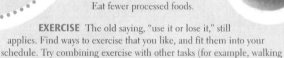

▶ **Balance.** Eat a variety of foods.

▶ **Moderation.** Don't eat too much or too often.

▶ **Natural.** Include foods that are in or close to their natural state. Eat fewer processed foods.

EXERCISE The old saying, "use it or lose it," still applies. Find ways to exercise that you like, and fit them into your schedule. Try combining exercise with other tasks (for example, walking with a study partner). Take advantage of:

▶ Local school and community athletic facilities
▶ Intramural programs for team sports
▶ Free exercise (walking or running outdoors, yoga at home)

SLEEP Students are often sleep deprived. However, research indicates that most brains need 8–9 hours a night to function well. Try to:

▶ Figure out how much sleep you need.
▶ Adjust your schedule and cut out low-priority commitments to free up sleep time.
▶ Avoid caffeine and alcohol late in the day/evening.
▶ Go to bed at a fairly consistent hour.

SUBSTANCES HAVE CONSEQUENCES

Although "self-medicating" with alcohol, drugs, or smoking can seem to take the edge off stress, the effect doesn't last—and using substances can have serious consequences. Make an informed choice.

ALCOHOL Moderation, moderation, moderation. Avoid *binge drinking* (more than 5 drinks at a sitting). Stay in control of your drinking and of what's in your glass.

DRUGS Different drugs carry a variety of damaging side effects, not the least of which is clouded judgment. Add in the fact that they are illegal and you could lose your student status—or more—and this becomes a highly problematic choice.

TOBACCO Regular smokers risk lung cancer and heart disease—and cigarettes are not cheap. You'll save cash and improve your health if you bypass this one.

PEOPLE CAN HELP

When the stress is getting to you, contact helpful resources such as the following (check your student handbook or institution website for e-mail addresses and phone numbers):

▶ Student health center
▶ Student counseling center
▶ Your academic advisor
▶ A trusted instructor or mentor

ALWAYS LEARNING

PEARSON

Succeeding in your Diverse World

DEFINING DIVERSITY

Diversity—the set of differences that exist among and within people—is a fact of modern life. Many students work, study, and live with people who differ from them in an enormous variety of ways, such as:

- Culture
- Ethnic origin
- Native language
- Race
- Gender
- Age
- Physical ability

Even in an environment where most people share the same culture and ethnic origin, diversity is just beneath the surface. Don't forget all the not-so-obvious but significant ways a person can differ from you:

- Socio-economic status
- Sexual orientation
- Religious beliefs
- Values
- Political affiliation
- Talents and interests

BE CULTURALLY INTELLIGENT

You may have heard of emotional intelligence—the ability to sense your own feelings and the feelings of others, understand them, and take them into account when deciding what to do or say. So what is *cultural intelligence?* Think of it as emotional intelligence with a cultural spin.

BE AWARE OF DIFFERENCES You don't have to work hard to notice traits such as skin color, spoken dialects, and culture-specific habits. Make an effort to note less visible differences.

UNDERSTAND DIFFERENCES As you work to understand the ways in which people differ from you, challenge your own judgments and assumptions.

- Through observation, questioning, and experience, learn more about the cultures around you.
- Don't assume that someone from a certain ethnic group has a skill or a deficit you associate with that group. Question your assumptions and try to move beyond them.
- Avoid judging a person's ability, intelligence, or intent based on a particular difference.

LET DIFFERENCES INFORM YOUR ACTIONS Interacting in a culturally intelligent way builds respect, forms lasting connections, and improves your chances of achieving any goal.

- Work to view situations from others' perspectives. For example, when a friend takes a position in an argument that is the total opposite of yours, take time to think about what is valid about her position.
- Respect values and traditions. For example, if a study group member avoids certain foods as part of his religious affiliation, make sure no one serves them at the group meeting.
- Adjust to language needs. Slow down your speech and avoid slang when interacting with someone who is not adept in the language you are speaking.

> **Cultural intelligence:** The ability to be aware of differences, understand them, and take them into account in your words and actions, all with the goal of functioning successfully in any situation regardless of the diverse people or perspectives involved.

> **" Diversity powers better problem solving. Diverse people = more ideas. "**

WHAT'S GOOD ABOUT . . .

. . . that much-younger or much-older student in your class? Listen to her comments for an interesting new perspective on course material.

. . . a friend from a different ethnic and/or cultural background? Challenge your perspectives and beliefs by learning about his. Explore aspects of an unfamiliar culture—food, language, religion, traditions.

. . . making an assumption about someone—and being wrong? Learning "the hard way" teaches you how to approach the next person with an open mind and reduces your willingness to jump to conclusions.

BE PART OF THE SOLUTION

CHALLENGE PREJUDICE
Although it is common to develop prejudices—literally, pre-judgments—based on experience and family influence, it is not helpful to hang on to them. Identify your prejudices, and analyze them critically. Do they make sense? Do they apply across the board? What are the consequences of applying them?

AVOID STEREOTYPING
A stereotype is an assumption about a person or group of people. Stereotypes are as common as prejudices—and as harmful. Think carefully about stereotypical ideas and try to set them aside. Look at each person as an individual.

FIGHT DISCRIMINATION
It is harmful and flat-out illegal to deny services to anyone based on age, race, ethnic origin, gender, religious affiliation, sexual orientation, potential or actual pregnancy, or potential or actual illness or disability. Don't do it—and report it if you see it.

Get Things Done with *Virtual Teams*

A NEW WAY TO LINK TO A TEAM

Technology hasn't changed the fact that success demands teamwork. However, it has changed the way that team members *connect*—electronically instead of in person—and that changes the game. Where do you find virtual teams?

VIRTUAL COLLEGE As a college student, you are on teams with your instructors, fellow students, and advisors. With online courses, most or all interactions will be virtual. Many traditional courses have some online component such as a course site on which you can post comments, e-mail your instructor, and submit work.

VIRTUAL WORKPLACE As an employee, you are on teams with co-workers and supervisors. Because working remotely saves time and money, more work teams are virtual. You will need to communicate and collaborate with teammates in different locations and time zones. Some virual teamwork tools:

▶ Skype (video chat with screen sharing ability)
▶ Campfirenow.com (group chat room that stores transcripts of meetings)
▶ Google docs (document collaboration tool)

SOCIAL NETWORKING With tools like Facebook or Google Groups, you can create a virtual team focused on any goal you choose—raising money for a cause, for example, or getting involved in politics in your neighborhood.

> " *The key to virtual team success is communication.* "

SUCCESS IN THE VIRTUAL WORKPLACE

Many of the strategies that help you in the virtual classroom carry over into the virtual workplace.

KNOW THE TECHNOLOGY. Ask your supervisor what technology you need to use to do your job. Then get trained on it. Companies usually offer training in the collaborative technologies they use to help their employees communicate and share materials.

STAY ON TOP OF TASKS. Just because no one can look over your cubicle wall doesn't mean you are any less accountable for achieving work goals. Set a schedule of tasks and stick to it.

FIND FACE TIME. No matter how easy it is to communicate virtually, face-to-face meetings are necessary from time to time. Occasional in-person meetings can help a team grow relationships, work through conflicts, and build positive energy together.

Keeping It Friendly Online

When you communicate through writing, you miss out on the information transmitted through tone of voice, facial expression, and body language. Here are some tips for staying civil with co-workers and classmates:

▶ Read over your comments/posts/blog entries before you hit "send." Make sure they don't sound rude, insulting, or harsh.
▶ Avoid all caps (IT READS LIKE YOU ARE SHOUTING).
▶ Use polite language liberally. *Please*, *thank you*, *appreciate*, and other respectful words and phrases go a long way.
▶ When it looks like e-mails are not getting the point across, pick up the phone and talk in real time.
▶ If you can, video chat using a program like Skype when you need a closer approximation to an in-person conversation.

SUCCESS IN THE VIRTUAL CLASSROOM

How can you work toward your goals in an online learning environment?

LEARN THE LMS. Your first task is to get up to speed on the LMS (learning management system) your course uses, as well as any other technologies you need to use to share documents or interact with classmates.

MANAGE YOURSELF. Self-motivation and discipline are crucial to online course success. Read your syllabus to understand course expectations. Set goals for yourself and pursue them step by step.

SET UP A SCHEDULE. Put important dates in your calendar—assignments due, quizzes and tests, online "meetings." If tasks don't have specific due dates, assign dates on your own.

COMMUNICATE WITH FELLOW STUDENTS. When you connect with the other students in the course, you build relationships that will make it easier to work together on projects or papers. Post questions, respond to comments, and share interesting videos or articles.

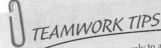

TEAMWORK TIPS

General teamwork strategies apply to any interaction, whether in-person or virtual.

▶ Set goals as a team.
▶ Get clear on your responsibilities.
▶ Do what you say you will do—on time.
▶ Ask questions when you are confused.
▶ Stay open-minded when considering ideas from others.
▶ Value diversity and avoid prejudice.

ALWAYS LEARNING   PEARSON

Civility

Paves the Way Toward Success

CIVILITY at a Glance

A BASIC DEFINITION

Civility (si-**vil**-i-tee), noun.
1. courtesy; politeness.
2. a polite action or expression.

MORE ABOUT CIVILITY

Civility is at the core of successful social interaction. It enables humans to build effective relationships, teams, and communities.

Civility incorporates these ideas:
- Treating others with respect
- Being considerate of the needs of others
- Conducting yourself with taste and restraint, and using self-discipline
- Avoiding being offensive to others
- Making choices that consider the needs of the community
- Behaving ethically (doing what's right)

ONLINE CIVILITY

Civil e-mails, texts, tweets, IMs, and online postings are just as important as civil in-person interactions. Why?

ELECTRONIC COMMUNICATION IS HERE TO STAY People text work colleagues, send Facebook messages to fellow students, e-mail instructors, and more. Communication is communication, no matter the venue, and civility should not be restricted to face-to-face interactions.

TONE IS AN ISSUE The tone of written electronic messages is easily misunderstood. When you can't see or hear a person, it can be hard to pick up on jokes, irony, or sarcasm.

EXTEND CIVILITY INTO THE ELECTRONIC REALM

General hints for any electronic communication:

- **Reread before you send.** Check your tone. Make sure that what you have written sounds clear and respectful and says what you want it to say.
- **Avoid all caps.** All caps convey SHOUTING.
- **Respond in a timely manner.** Some e-mails require quicker responses than others. Make sure you get back to the sender in a time period appropriate to the subject of the e-mail.
- **Remember that words can travel.** Anything you write can be copied and forwarded. Think carefully before you hit *send*: Does what you have written reflect well on you?

> " *Civility builds relationships with people who will help you achieve your goals.* "

If you are writing an instructor, advisor, work supervisor, or other authority:

- **Use proper titles.** Address your recipient with the appropriate title and level of formality.
  - **Use respectful greetings and closings.** "Dear Ms. Thompson" is preferable to "Hey Ms. T," and "Sincerely" or "Regards" is better than "gtg."
  - **Use full sentences, good grammar, and correct punctuation.** Write as you would for any work task or class assignment.
  - **Don't underestimate the power of politeness.** "Please," "thank you," "I appreciate it," and other courteous words make a difference.
- **Avoid emoticons.** Save emoticons and clip-art images for social e-mails and texts.

CIVILITY: Not Just for the Other Person

Being civil is not just about what you do for others. It benefits you in ways essential to success in school and out.

CIVILITY BUILDS COMMUNITY Interacting civilly with members of your communities—at your school, workplace, home, online—helps build relationships. How well a community functions comes down to whether individuals can connect successfully.

CIVILITY CREATES (OR RESTORES) TRUST

Trust is at the heart of any productive relationship. When you trust someone, you can benefit from their help in achieving your goals.

CIVILITY IMPROVES YOUR HEALTH Really? Yes, really. Research shows that when you interact civilly with others, your body produces chemicals that reduce aggressive feelings, stimulate brain function, and increase cooperation. On the other hand, uncivil behavior results in surges of stress hormones that can depress your immune system and increase blood pressure.

Avoid! Avoid!

Your time in school is valuable (and expensive!), so spend it learning. Contribute to a positive learning environment by avoiding these uncivil actions.

1. Insulting an instructor or fellow student (in person, via e-mail, or in a posting)
2. Cheating—either on tests or by turning in someone else's work
3. Interacting inappropriately with the instructor or students (interrupting, challenging aggressively, belittling others' ideas)
4. Using language that is unacceptable in the classroom
5. Talking or texting on a cell phone during class
6. Focusing on diversions during class (newspapers, online articles, personal appearance) that have nothing to do with the material being presented or discussed
7. Talking with other students during the lecture
8. Arriving to class late, or leaving early, without a compelling reason
9. Sharing jokes, videos, or other materials with someone who might take offense
10. Littering or defacing campus property

Maintaining Your Financial Sanity

Paying attention to your savings, spending, and borrowing choices means more financial sanity *now* as well as after graduation. Ask questions. Read fine print. And, know where your money is and where it goes.

MANAGING STUDENT LOANS

EXPLORE OPTIONS BEFORE YOU TAKE ON DEBT

Contact your financial aid office to learn about aid that does not need to be repaid, such as:

- *Scholarships* (awards based on merit and requiring a certain criteria)
- *Grants* (money given by government or private agencies, usually based on financial need)

Always ask. Don't assume you can't get aid.

FEDERAL LOANS FIRST, PRIVATE LOANS SECOND

If you must borrow, seek federal loans first. Why?

- ▸ **Better Rates:** Federal loans have lower interest rates than private ones.
- ▸ **Better Repayment**: Federal borrowers may qualify for Income-Based Repayment (IBR), a program that caps loan payments based on income and family size, and forgives remaining student loan debt after 25 years of payments.
- ▸ **Loan Forgiveness:** With the U.S. Dept. of Education's Public Service Loan Forgiveness (PSLF) program, the Feds will forgive part of a federal loan if the borrower makes 120 on-time payments while working full time for 10 years at a "public service" employer such as a non-profit, AmeriCorps, or a government entity (military, public schools, etc.). The forgiveness applies to debt that remains after the 10 years of work.
- ▸ **FAFSA (Free Application for Federal Student Aid):** You must reapply every year for federal aid (www.fafsa.ed.gov) using the FAFSA form.

DO THE MATH Learn now what you'll owe later.

Step 1: If you have a loan, speak with your loan officer. Find out how much you'll owe per month and for how long.

Step 2: Estimate your first-year salary and deduct 1/3 (for taxes). Then divide what remains by 12 to see your projected monthly take-home pay.

Step 3: Compare your take-home pay and your monthly loan payments. Ask: *Can I make the minimum loan payments comfortably?*

MANAGING DAY-TO-DAY SPENDING

NEEDS vs WANTS If you prioritize needs over wants, you'll get a better grip on your spending.

Need: If you can't live without it to function in society, it's a need.
Examples: Housing, food, childcare.

Want: If you can shrug it off, it's a want.
Examples: dining out, music and movie downloads, an extra pair of jeans.

STICK TO CASH Studies show we save money (up to 20%) when we use cash, because it's harder to part with cash than to swipe a credit card. Seeing bills leave your wallet can make you think twice about buying those movie tickets or that mocha latte.

KEEP TRACK For a week, jot down your daily purchases in your phone, PDA, or notebook. Then, look at how and where you spend your money.

Analyze what changes can help you spend less and save more.

GET DISCOUNTS Don't leave home without your student ID. Student discounts mean instant savings on food, computers, entertainment, and more. For other coupons, try the "Coupon Sherpa" free smart-phone app.

STAY ON TOP OF YOUR BANK BALANCE Your ATM receipt doesn't always show an accurate bank balance. Check your account activity and balance regularly via the Web or phone. Use personal finance software like Quicken to balance your checking account monthly. Mobile phone applications like Mint (free) and Spend (cost: 99 cents) can also help you track spending.

> " *Let's be real: credit cards feel like free money.* "

MANAGING CREDIT CARDS

The average college student graduates with about $4,000 in credit card debt. Yikes! If you choose to use a credit card, do so responsibly.

UNDERSTAND APR *(Annual Percentage Rate)*. APR is the amount of interest you pay for the use of credit (unless you pay the entire balance every month). The average APR on a standard credit card is about 15%, according to Bankrate.com. **Psst:** Credit unions offer cards with some of the lowest APRs around.

GO BEYOND THE MINIMUM PAYMENT *(the amount creditors require you to pay each month)*. Paying only the minimum traps you into forking out more interest on what you still owe. If you can, pay your balance in full each month. If you can't, at least try to pay double or triple the minimum.

PAY ON TIME Card companies charge hefty fees for late payments. If your payment is due on the 30th of each month, set an alarm in your phone or an e-mail alert as a reminder to pay the bill on time. If you can rely on having funds available, try setting up auto-payments with your credit card company or bank.

PEARSON

Protect *your* Personal Data

The more you do online, the greater the chance that your privacy may be compromised.

> *Minimize risk through privacy settings, privacy technology, and careful choices.*

YOU LIVE IN A PUBLIC WORLD

Sharing information electronically makes that information readily available to others. Above all, know this: The privacy of your personal information and electronic communication is not guaranteed. Normal, day-to-day actions put your privacy at risk:

- E-mails and postings on discussion boards or in chat rooms can be forwarded.

- Sites where you shop online track your purchases and even what you look at when browsing, and can share that information with other companies.

- Status updates, postings, photos, and videos on social networking sites can be viewed by people who do not know you.

- Search engines often keep electronic logs of the sites you access and use that information to target particular advertising to you.

BE CAREFUL ABOUT WHAT YOU WRITE

Anything that you write and send electronically has the potential to travel beyond your intended recipient. If you want to keep a message or conversation private, talk in person or make a phone call.

- **E-mails.** Think before you write. E-mail can easily be forwarded to someone else, with or without your knowledge or consent.

- **Social networking site postings.** Whatever you write and post on a site can be copied and pasted elsewhere. If you don't want the whole world to know something, don't put it on your status update.

- **Chat room or discussion board notes.** First of all, consider using a pseudonym when visting a non-academic chat room or discussion board. Secondly, keep all personal information out of these discussions. You can't know with whom you are communicating and how they might use your information.

- **Texts.** Text messages you send can be copied, traced, and forwarded—or even just shown to someone else.

PRIVACY POLICIES AND SETTINGS

Nearly every website you can register on, whether a business, organization, or social networking site, has a privacy policy. Most also have ways you can adjust your privacy settings.

READ PRIVACY POLICIES Privacy information is often in fine print in the corner of the site. Search for it and read it so that you know what information the site can gather about you and what rights you have to manage your information.

CUSTOMIZE PRIVACY SETTINGS Exercise your rights. For example, you can indicate that you don't want a company to share your information with sister companies, or make sure the photos you post on Facebook are available to your friends only.

MANAGE PERSONAL COMPUTER SETTINGS Many sites you visit will put "cookies" on your computer—small bits of software that store your personal information and allow you to easily return to and navigate the site. However, cookies can also be used to track purchases or collect information. You can set your computer to reject all cookies or to alert you each time a site wants to send you a cookie.

Privacy COMMON SENSE

It's challenging to keep up with the ever-changing world of electronic communication and information. Stick with these strategies and you can't go wrong.

- **When in doubt, opt out.** If you are not sure about whether you want information to be shared or you want to receive communications from a site online, vote no. Look for "opt out" procedures on banking and shopping sites.

- **Keep your data to yourself.** Do not electronically post or send your phone numbers, address, Social Security number, birth date, credit card numbers, bank account numbers, or institution name. Remember, anything you write has the potential to be captured.

- **Stick with people you know.** Avoid accepting people as online "friends" unless you've met them in person first. Never reveal any personal information to a stranger in a chat room or on a discussion board.

- **Bank and shop safely.** If a website has proper security, you will see a small padlock at the bottom of the page where you are instructed to enter credit card or bank information. Additionally, the web address of that page should have an "s" after the "http" (it signifies "security").

ALWAYS LEARNING   PEARSON

Strategy and Tactics for Military Students

> *Succeeding in college is like a military campaign. Plan well and leverage your military skills to reach your educational goals.*

GET FINANCIAL AID

ACTIVE DUTY SERVICE MEMBERS
You are eligible for tuition assistance (TA) through your branch of service. Visit your base education center or your branch of service Web portal for more information, such as www.GoArmyEd.com.

VETERANS AND ELIGIBLE ACTIVE DUTY SERVICE MEMBERS The Post 9/11 GI Bill and previous versions are a key source of tuition aid for those who qualify: See http://www.gibill.va.gov/. Some schools supplement the GI Bill with money through the Yellow Ribbon program. Visit your school's website to find out more.

NATIONAL GUARD Search the National Guard website for your state for financial aid help. Some states even offer free in-state tuition.

ROTC An ROTC scholarship will pay for tuition, books, and fees. Even if you're not on scholarship, you may still be able to receive money if you participate in ROTC programs.

OTHER SCHOLARSHIPS Search for other scholarships from sources such as Officer's Wives clubs and the American Legion.

CHOOSE THE RIGHT SCHOOL

Searching for a military-friendly school? Find an accredited school and rate these key areas:

The school...	NEVER				ALWAYS
Understands my lifestyle and challenges.	1	2	3	4	5
Maximizes credit transfer to/from other schools AND gives credit for military training and experience.	1	2	3	4	5
Allows for unexpected absences, such as giving extra time to submit work when military duty interferes.	1	2	3	4	5
Offers many support services.	1	2	3	4	5
Offers the degree program I want.	1	2	3	4	5

The higher the rating, the friendlier the school.

HINT: For online courses, you should also find out what classroom login requirements are. Asynchronous log in (no requirement to be in class at a specific time) is best if you expect absences.

GET AS MUCH CREDIT AS YOU CAN

You probably have more credit hours than you think, even if you've never been to college. Military training and experience is often worth academic credit.

▸ Find out the school policy on credit for military training or experience.

▸ Provide school officials a copy of your military training/education record; the American Council on Education (ACE) can help you get your transcript: www.acenet.edu/AM/Template.cfm?Section=Military_Programs

▸ Consider taking tests for credit: CLEP and DANTES are two good sources.

▸ Research your school's prior learning assessment policy on receiving credit for knowledge you've gained through volunteer work, hobbies, home businesses, and other activities.

BEWARE: Not all credits you've earned will transfer. Talk to your advisor early to find out which ones will.

CLASSROOM TACTICS

The tactics of hard work and discipline will help you succeed. Put them to use by approaching college as you would a military operation:

THE MISSION Understand course and program requirements, and know what success looks like.

▸ Read the syllabus to familiarize yourself with upcoming assignments, grading policies, and deadlines.

▸ Know what the learning objectives are for each course, and how your learning will be assessed.

THE COMMANDER Follow the orders of your instructors and give them what they want.

▸ Complete your assignments on time and do them exactly as directed.

▸ Participate actively in class, whether online or face to face. Show the instructor you want to be a good student; it will help at grading time.

ALLIES Create support groups to share intelligence and get help.

▸ Find other military students, especially those who are in your classes or academic program.

▸ Use veterans groups, social networks, clubs, and organizations to your advantage.

▸ Don't ignore the library; librarians love to help with research and can be the link to support services.

LEADERSHIP: Chances are, you have some leadership experience. Use your skills to take a lead role with projects, run for office in the student government, or volunteer to lead campus activities (even online!). You will get from your school experience what you put into it.

ALWAYS LEARNING

PEARSON

Appendix C
Professional Readiness

Resources Are All Around You • Career Readiness
• Create Your Personal Brand • Building Your Professional Image

Resources
All Around You

Tuition fees don't just pay for coursework. You are also buying access to resources that help you make the most of your time in school. Get more bang for your buck—make your campus resources work for you.

Success

FINANCIAL AID

Finding, applying for, and securing financial aid can be a major undertaking. Counselors and other staff at your school's financial aid office can help you every step of the way.

FIND AID Research loans, grants, and scholarships using books, brochures, and websites. Staff members can guide your search. Tell them about yourself and ask their advice—they may know about grants or scholarships you are eligible for that you have never heard of.

APPLY FOR AID Staff members can help you fill out forms for loans, grants, and scholarships, including the FAFSA (Free Application for Federal Student Aid) form required for all federal loans and grants.

KNOW YOUR SCHOOL Your financial aid office can get you up to speed on your school's payment requirements—costs, types of aid for which students at your school are eligible, work-study programs available, when payments are due and how they're submitted, and more.

MANAGE YOUR MONEY Many schools offer online access to your account so that you can track payments and financial aid awards and see what you owe in fees and loans. Some financial aid offices offer general money management help.

ACADEMIC HELP

Here are ideas for finding support in your quest for academic success.

ADVISING

▶ **Academic advisors.** You will be assigned an academic advisor who will help you choose courses, plan a major, and move toward your degree. Generally you meet with your advisor once per term, but don't hesitate to ask for help whenever you need it.

▶ **Instructors.** Every course syllabus lists your instructor's office hours—schedule a meeting to ask questions. Send a polite e-mail (and give your instructor at least 24 hours to respond).

▶ **Departments.** If you want to know more about a particular major, talk with the department secretary or schedule a meeting with an instructor in that department.

ACADEMIC CENTERS

Many institutions have *academic skills centers* (places where you can go for resources, support, or tutoring in skills). Look for your school's:

▶ Math Center
▶ Writing Center
▶ Reading Center

Some schools also have *academic centers* (facilities focused on helping students majoring in a particular area). Search "academic center" on your school's website to see what it offers.

JOB AND CAREER RESOURCES

Get help with **work now** (job placement office) and **work later** (career planning and placement center).

JOB PLACEMENT OFFICE Visit this office to check out job opportunities both on and off campus. Staff can help you access online and hard copy resources, sort through listings, and fill out applications.

CAREER PLANNING AND PLACEMENT CENTER Visit this center to access written and online resources as well as services such as:

▶ Career counseling
▶ Personal interest assessments
▶ Internship placement
▶ Resume-building assistance
▶ Help with post-graduation job searches and applications

HELP IS WAITING IF YOU NEED . . .

RESIDENTIAL OR COMMUTER SERVICES Residents, get help with housing issues such as heating and cooling, safety, and room-mates. Commuters, find transportation and carpools and handle issues such as parking and weather updates.

COUNSELING OR HEALTH SERVICES At nearly every institution, students can enroll in the school's health plan. Counseling offices provide mental health support (therapy, support groups, substance abuse treatment, and more). Health services may include athletic facilities.

ASSISTANCE WITH TECHNOLOGY Locate your school's computer center or help desk (in person or on the website) for assistance with your e-mail account, online resources, or computers.

INDIVIDUAL SUPPORT Look for services for students with physical or learning disabilities, cultural organizations, religious services, mentoring programs, and more.

HELP

STAY SAFE

Reach out to . . .

▶ **Campus Security.** Put the campus security number on speed-dial. Call if you see or experience a problem.

▶ **Tech Support.** Sign up to receive alerts via e-mail or phone. Ask for help if you receive questionable e-mails.

▶ **Instructors.** Get help if you have a problem with a fellow student.

▶ **Late-night Support.** If your school has a "walking service," ask a volunteer to walk you home.

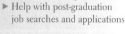
ALWAYS LEARNING

PEARSON

Career Readiness
Get Ready for Workplace Success!

The Modern Workplace Runs on TECHNOLOGY

Almost any job will require some basic level of technological ability. Make sure you can:

- Communicate on e-mail and/or by text
- Use a word-processing program such as Microsoft Word
- Perform an online information search
- Fulfill any technological requirements specific to that job (i.e., computer programs, machine operation)

CREATE A RESUME THAT GETS NOTICED

The goal of the resume: To sell **you**. Your resume is a marketing tool, and you are the product. How can you get started?

CHOOSE A FORMAT Give your resume a modern look. Instructors or professionals may have advice about formats that are commonly used in certain careers.

MAKE A FIRST DRAFT Put your information into the format you've chosen. Then get feedback from people you trust.

LESS IS MORE If you can, stick with one page—two pages maximum. Avoid word overload—have "white space" on your page to make it easier to read. Use bullets and short phrases.

USE KEYWORDS If you know the career area you are aiming for, include *keywords* from that area. The more keywords, the more likely your resume will be picked up by an employer's electronic scanner.

GET HELP AT THE CAREER CENTER Consult with a career counselor on format; solicit feedback on a draft; look for help with targeting your resume to a specific career area.

SMART JOB SEARCHING

With your resume ready to go, prepare for a successful job search.

GET YOUR SYSTEM READY How will you keep track of submissions, interviews, responses? Set up a system that works for you—on paper, on your smartphone, on your computer.

STOCK YOUR MATERIALS Print resumes on quality paper (a heavier weight than printer paper). Get some stationery for hard-copy follow-up notes. Have the electronic version of your resume saved and ready to send out.

USE JOB SEARCH SITES Use search engines to find the most up-to-date job search sites. Get advice at the career center on which sites are most effective (or best for your particular career area).

MINE YOUR CONNECTIONS Connect with your network to see what you can find. Get the word out to friends and family; send e-mails and post on Facebook; use networking sites like LinkedIn.

> ❝ *The two building blocks of career readiness: teamwork and critical thinking.* ❞

Build the Skills Employers *Want!*

Your work in school gives you the ability to read, write, and do basic math—important for workplace success, but that is just the starting point. What else do you need?

TRANSFERABLE SKILLS

A *transferable skill* is a general skill useful in any job (and transferable from one job to another). Teamwork, for example, is just as important for a marine biologist as it is for a high school teacher. You'll need these skills in any workplace environment:

- **Teamwork and cultural competence:** working respectfully and effectively with others, no matter how they differ from you

- **Critical thinking and problem solving:** analyzing situations, brainstorming ideas, choosing and implementing solutions
- **Creativity:** thinking out of the box about problems and coming up with new ideas
- **Responsibility:** doing what you say you will do
- **Communication:** being able to communicate effectively in writing and in person
- **Goals:** setting a goal and working toward it successfully
- **Leadership:** taking the lead when the situation demands
- **Ethics and integrity:** doing what's right, relating to others with honesty, and being true to your word

- **Lifelong learning:** showing a commitment to continual learning on the job
- **Flexibility:** being able to adjust to change

JOB-SPECIFIC SKILLS

Prospective employees need to demonstrate the skills the job requires. The technical skills needed for some jobs are more obvious than others—for example, nurses need specific medical training. When you investigate any job, find out the specific technical skills required. Make sure you have them under your belt before you apply.

ALWAYS LEARNING · PEARSON

Create Your Personal BRAND

WHAT IS PERSONAL BRANDING?

When someone mentions the electronic brand Apple, you probably think of cutting-edge products and technology. This is the goal of *branding*—to create a name or **brand**, link it to a **product**, and market it so that the name communicates value. *Personal branding* means applying this process to **yourself**:

- ▶ Your name is the brand, and you are the product.
- ▶ You market your brand to potential employers.
- ▶ Your skills, talents, and abilities show the value of the product.

Standing out in the crowd of the modern workplace and finding the right job fit demands that you market yourself effectively. Make that happen through the process of personal branding.

1. See yourself as a product to be marketed.
2. Determine what is unique and valuable about your product.
3. Market your product.
4. Make careful choices, knowing that everything you do reflects on your product.

> " *Standing out in the crowd of the modern workplace demands that you market yourself effectively.* "

DEFINE YOUR PRODUCT LINE

You are the product in the spotlight. What are your key features? Just as Apple promotes the latest capabilities of the iPhone, you can define and promote your unique and desirable qualities as an employee.

EVALUATE YOUR TALENTS AND ABILITIES Your most promotable features are the things you do well. Consider both specific skills (such as nursing) and transferable skills that apply to any job (problem solving).

CONSIDER YOUR GOALS Look at what you want from your education and your career, and frame your talents and abilities in the context of these long-term goals.

LOOK AT HOW PEOPLE PERCEIVE YOU Ask friends, family, and your instructors what they see as your strong points. What people think is valuable about you will help you define your product.

Now put it all together: Create a product description

Thinking about your abilities, goals, and how you are perceived, write a paragraph or list of key features for Brand "You." Focus only on your strengths and what you think will showcase you best.

SELLING BRAND "you"

- ▶ **Gather marketing materials.** Create a focused, updated resume. Include a phone number and e-mail address that people can use to contact you. Make business cards— you can design them online in no time and have them sent to you.

  - ▶ **Be visible.** Promote yourself in person with friends, family, work associates, or faculty who might be able to help you. Use online services like LinkedIn to define and advertise yourself. Volunteer for tasks that show off your talents.

- ▶ **Promote "seals of approval."** Just as a package might announce how a product won an award, Brand "You" can display seals of approval. Make degrees, awards, and other accomplishments prominent on your resume. Talk about them in interviews, on cover letters, and in follow-up communication.

- ▶ **Keep up with product development.** If there is an area of skill you need to build, do it. Read, take a course, join an organization, sign up for a workshop. The modern workplace needs lifelong learners.

EVERYTHING REFLECTS ON YOUR BRAND

Having a great experience with an iMac can make you think Apple is great. On the other hand, suffering through an iPod glitch can lower your opinion of the whole company. This is also true of Brand "You." Everything visible about you—in person as well as your electronic presence—makes a statement. How can you make sure the statement is positive?

- ▶ **Dress appropriately.** Anywhere you want to promote your brand—in the classroom, on the job, in an interview, at a meeting—your appearance makes an impression. Put some effort into it.

- ▶ **Manage social networking.** Potential employers can access Facebook pages, sign up for tweets, and read blogs. Anything electronically linked to your name needs to show you in a positive light.

- ▶ **Be on your best behavior.** How you speak, treat others, and behave matters. And it all gets noticed. Respectful, positive behavior will go a long way toward promoting your brand effectively.

ALWAYS LEARNING

PEARSON

Building Your Professional IMAGE

FIRST IMPRESSIONS

If a picture is worth a thousand words, the image you present in an interview says a lot. Dress, manners, body language, and voice combine to create a picture of *you*. Employers evaluate that snapshot the moment you walk into your interview.

PUT TOGETHER THE RIGHT LOOK FOR THE INTERVIEW

▶ Dress a bit more formally than the daily wear of those with whom you hope to work. It signals respect.

▶ Avoid anything too casual such as T-shirts, jeans, sneakers, or flip-flops.

▶ Make sure what you wear is clean and ironed and fits well.

▶ Choose clothing comfortable enough that you don't fidget.

▶ Get cleaned up and keep your hair under control. For women, makeup adds a nice touch, but don't overdo it. Good grooming is a must!

▶ Make sure your shoes are clean and not worn out. People notice shoes.

▶ Check yourself from head to toe after you've finished dressing. Is your tie straight? Belt centered? Collar even?

▶ Keep it simple. Class, not flash, should be your guide.

> " *Create an image that matches your ambition.* "

BRAND YOURSELF

To go beyond the first impression and make a *lasting* impression on the job, identify and develop your skills, qualities, and unique talents. Learn what makes you stand out. Promote yourself . . . as "Brand You."

"BRAND YOU" CHECKLIST

❑ Think and learn more about your skills, strengths, and interests. (Assessments such as the Golden Interest Inventory can help.)

❑ Build a network of people who appreciate your skills and strengths and are willing to talk about them.

❑ Identify how you are uniquely valuable to an employer.

❑ Find ways to make your value visible without seeming arrogant.

❑ Take on challenges. Take risks.

❑ Always do quality work . . . no matter the task.

❑ Help others succeed.

❑ Continue to find new ways to improve your value.

❑ Be able to demonstrate you did the items on this list.

OTHER IMAGE TIPS

▶ Make sure nails, hair, piercings, and other jewelry are appropriate for the job environment.

▶ Make eye contact. Smile when introduced.

▶ Lean slightly forward. Look alert. Listen well.

▶ Shut off your cell phone during interviews.

▶ Say "please" and "thank you," and hold the elevator door open. Manners matter.

▶ Brush up on your dining etiquette if you'll be eating during the interview.

BE PROFESSIONAL IN E-MAIL, TEXTS, AND SOCIAL NETWORKS

What Goes Around May Come Back Around: Post with care. Employers often look online (from Facebook and Twitter to Google) during background checks of potential employees.

With friends and strangers . . .

▶ Think carefully about what you write or post.

▶ Wait 24 hours if you are emotional about a topic. Ask: *What effect would that nasty post or Tweet have on your image if a potential employer reads it?*

With potential employers . . .

▶ Online communication should reflect good writing skills. Use clear, business-like language.

▶ Stay away from sarcasm and jokes. They tend not to translate well in writing.

▶ Avoid abbreviations and emoticons. Instead of "K" or "BTW," try "yes" and "by the way."

▶ Always check for errors in spelling or grammar before sending.

▶ Send a thank you in an e-mail or written note after interviews, not a text. And don't post a message on your profile saying "nailed the interview."

KEEP YOUR PERSONAL INFORMATION PRIVATE

SOCIAL NETWORKS

Confused by the privacy rules? No surprise. These sites make money from selling your information, so providing privacy is not their first priority. Your job is to:

▶ Read and understand privacy policies for the social media you use. Ask questions to clear up confusion.

▶ Adjust security settings so you only reveal information and visuals you would show to the general public.

▶ Consider having two profiles—one for friends and one for the public (including future employers).

▶ When in doubt, keep information private.

PRIVACY ISSUES IN FORUMS/CHAT ROOMS

Everything you write can be copied and saved, and you don't really know who is posting. Only post what you'd be willing to show an employer. Choose a screen name not traceable to you or to your regular e-mail address.

ALWAYS LEARNING   PEARSON

Answer Key for Selected Items

Additional Questions – Even-numbered Items

Chapter 3: Observing and Remembering

Alejandrez, "Cesar Chavez Saved My Life"
2. a   4. a

Petry, "The Wind Catcher"
2. a   4. c

Bovard, "The Red Chevy"
2. d   4. a

Chapter 4: Reading Critically, Analyzing Rhetorically

McGrath, "Rhetorical Analysis of Gregory Petsko's Open Letter to George M. Philip"
2. d   4. c

Koester and Browe, "Two Responses to Deborah Tannen"
2. d   4. a

Chapter 5: Analyzing and Designing Visuals

Lewis, "Some Don't Like Their Blues At All"
2. d   4. d

Chapter 6: Investigating

Macke, "Permanent Tracings"
2. c   4. d

Chapter 7: Explaining

Orman, "How To Take Control of Your Credit Cards"
2. c   4. b

Tannen, "How Male and Female Students Use Language Differently""
2. a   4. d

Blakely, "White Lies: White-Collar Crime in America"
2. b   4. b

Brosseau, "Anorexia Nervosa"
2. b   4. c

Chapter 8: Evaluating

Sedaris, "Today's Special"
2. c   4. a

Klockeman, "Vulgar Propriety"
2. c   4. d

Chapter 9: Problem Solving

Arum, "Your So-Called Education"
2. d   4. a

O'Shaughnessy, "But Can They Write?"
2. d   4. b

Surowiecki, "Debt By Degrees"
2. b   4. c

Leonhardt, "Even for Cashiers, College Pays Off"
2. a   4. b

Petsko, "An Open Letter to George M. Philip…"
2. b   4. d

Tannen, "The Argument Culture"
2. d   4. a

Richman, "Can Citizen Journalism Pick Up the Pieces?"
2. d   4. a

Chapter 10: Arguing

Cleaver, "The Internet: A Clear and Present Danger?"
2. a   4. c

Manjoo, "You Have No Friends"
2. c   4. d

Kliff, "And Why I Hate It…"
2. b   4. b

Holladay, "Cyberbullying"
2. b   4. a

Boyd and Marwick, "Bullying as True Drama"
2. c   4. c

Helft, "Facebook Wrestles with Free Speech and Civility"
2. a   4. c

Waters, "Why You Can't Cite Wikipedia in My Class"
2. a   4. d

Wilson, "Professors Should Embrace Wikipedia"
2. c   4. c

Carr, "Does the Internet Make You Dumber?"
2. c   4. b

Sabatke, "Welfare Is Still Necessary for Women and Children in the U.S."
2. d   4. d

Chapter 11: Responding to Literature

Bambara, "The Lesson"
2. d   4. a

Five Contemporary Poems
2. b   4. c

Rexroth: "Facing It: Reflection on War"
2. b   4. c

Russell: "Death: The Final Freedom"
2. b   4. c